Energy Almanac

Astrological Insights & Holistic Resources for The Year Ahead

P U B L I S H I N G
fun. fresh. transformational.

Published by Big Sky Publishing, LLC
Edited by Susan Puiia
Design by Kendra Cagle, 5 Lakes Design

ISBN-13: 978-0-578-56351-0

www.shopBigSky.com

Dedication
◇◇◇

For all the beautiful people who
want to connect the dots.
This is for you.

"Keep your eyes on the stars and your feet on the ground."

- Theodore Roosevelt, 26th President

From the Publisher

I'm sure I shouldn't have been surprised to find myself swooped by an owl that day. She came directly at me, quite unexpectedly, as I sat waiting to pull out onto the highway after delivering a spiritually powerful workshop about the energies of 2019. The "Treehouse" studio, aptly named, was on the third floor. It indeed offered a bird's-eye view of the nearby landscape. The owl must have been guarding that treehouse as the group absorbed information. When she demanded my attention by diving directly at me from 50 feet across the highway, the message was clear.

Intuition kicked in and I knew in an instant what she needed.

The owl, harbinger of change, was talking about the year ahead. 2020. Wow! I made the short drive home and sped to my office to start taking notes on the thoughts that were now pouring in. I researched totem animals. It had been a few years since Owl had shown herself to me, but we surely weren't unfamiliar with one another.

Magic. Change. Wisdom. Intuition. Silence. The gift of sight and uncovering what's hidden. I believe owl bears the message of everything that 2020 holds. Owl demanded her presence on the cover of what would be the 2020 Energy Almanac.

Weave the message of the Owl totem with the 2020 movement of the planets and you have an incredible map of energies to guide the year ahead.

Please enjoy your Energy Almanac which is filled to the brim with incredible information. Find the voice of the contributors you love and join them on social media for more guidance and support. Their individual biographies are in the resource section in the back of this book. Be sure to tag us in your own social media posts and let us know how your 2020 is shaping up; use hashtags #EnergyAlmanac, #AstroInklings, #PlanByThePlanets.

May your 2020 be filled with magic and insight.

TAM VEILLEUX
COACH, CREATIVE, & PUBLISHER

VIRGO

BIG SKY PUBLISHING LLC

TAURUS

 www.shopBigSky.com

About Astrology

Names, numbers, and astrology are but clues to a big game. The game board itself is your life. The piece moving across that board is you: the top hat, shoe, ship or flat iron (all yours if you love Monopoly). The moveable playing piece represents you and your innate wiring, your personal astrology, numerology, habits, traits, nature (see the Project Evolve article) and genetics. Your personal astrology is represented in your birth sign, also called your sun or zodiac sign. Clues to how you might move through your days, weeks, months and years (the gameboard) can be guided by certain cards you draw (your birth name) and by the roll of the dice (numerology).

With all of this insight available to you the question is, do you study the gameboard, cards, and dice to understand the game more fully, or do you blindly roll the dice and move your marker across the board willy-nilly hoping for the best?

Astrology, according to Wikipedia, is *"the study of the movements and relative positions of celestial objects as a means for divining information about human affairs and terrestrial events."* Around since the second millennium and used by some of the ancient world's greatest thinkers like Aratus, Ptolemy, Thomas Aquinas, and Roger Bacon, humans have long been able to see the relationship between events on earth and the corresponding location of specific planets. So, what's to stop modern man and woman from using the heavens as a way of predicting life events? Answer: nothing.

In our current world of smartphones, artificial intelligence, and Bluetooth technology, we tend to google the answers to our biggest challenges. We post a selfie on Instagram of our shock or grief and a sarcastic meme to facebook about our unrest. We forget that for some solid answers to life's most perplexing questions, we need only look to names, numbers, and astrology.

To this writer, astrology can be both predictive and reflective. Through looking back to the astrology at play during an integral moment in our lives, we're able to connect the dots to the events that played out. Looking ahead, it's easy to see what's coming and how to address the topic with grace.

Knowing how the planets are positioned and what the meaning is behind that position offers amazing insight to what may play out. In the 2020 edition of The Energy Almanac, our goal is to help you in the game of life because when playing a game, it's good to have a strategy.

✴ www.shopBigSky.com ✴

About Astrology and This Almanac

The Energy Almanac as a regular reference can help you in making decisions. It will share with you insight as to the more global movements that you might experience in the months ahead. "Forewarned is forearmed," someone once said, and isn't that the truth?

WE SUGGEST THREE STEPS FOR USING YOUR 2020 ALMANAC:

First, as you move through the 12 months making up 2020, give this publication regular readings. Read through once for a solid overview of what's happening this year. Highlight pieces of information that intrigue you. Create a list of relative dates and events before giving the book a second reading. During the second reading, underline pertinent pieces that will affect your personal decision making. Add any dates and information from these initial reads into your personal calendaring system for the year.

Secondly, read the Almanac monthly and weekly. At the start of the month, pull out the art and pin it nearby. It's a reflection tool meant to be seen and referenced often. Be cognizant of which aspects and transits are highlighted each week and how you might need to traverse them relative to your own game of life. Place The Energy Almanac itself in a conspicuous location where you will bump into it regularly. Pick one day each week to interact with this information.

Lastly, break your mother's rule. Write in this book. If you know you have upcoming travel, decisions to make, health issues to face in 2020, jot these things down weekly or monthly and reread the printed insights. Let the information guide you. As the days and weeks pass, write the results of your week. You will begin to connect the dots about your own personal relationship to the planets. Remember to capture the more global goings on,. Pay attention to politics, education, medicine, weather. It's all impacted by the movements of the planets.

Use the holistic resources as suggested by our hand-picked experts in their field. From numerology and gemstones to movement, oils, and journaling and nourishment suggestions, you have an entire collection of tools at your fingertips for 2020.

You are invited to play the game of life at a whole new level. Connect the dots and see what may be ahead for you. Earthly happenings can be foretold, and it starts by looking at the heavens. Theodore Roosevelt, 26th President of the United States of America, knew this. He said, "Keep your eyes on the stars and your feet on the ground."

The planets have a plan for you and The Energy Almanac reveals them all. Plan accordingly.

✴ www.shopBigSky.com ✴

How the Planets Play

PLANETS

Recall, if you will, the Roman myths we learned. Think of the ten planets as actors from those tales. Each planet is named after a character in a story with its own personality and traits. For example, in mythology, Saturn was the god of time and taught agriculture to his people. Saturn rules time, karma, discipline, and responsibility.

SATURN

ZODIAC SIGNS

The twelve zodiac signs can be thought of as pieces of clothing that the planets might wear for a period of time. Each sign has specific qualities, traits, strengths, weaknesses, and general attitudes toward life. When a planet is traversing in any specific sign, its own personality will be affected by the qualities of the sign. Example: The zodiac sign of Virgo is known for being analytical, health oriented, mentally astute, detailed, preachy, overwhelmed, self-critical, and uptight.

SATURN IN VIRGO

ASTROLOGICAL HOUSES

The twelve houses of astrology represent where the character of the story will be. It's the stage or scene they will act in. The houses relate to internal areas such as values, wishes, goals, and shadow work, as well as more external and tangible areas such as children, money, religion, and career. As a planet moves through a house, that area of life will feel the pressure of said planet.

SATURN IN VIRGO IN THE 5TH HOUSE OF CHILDREN & CREATIVITY

ASPECTS

Aspects speak to how exactly the characters will play together based on where they are located. Maybe they'll be kind to one another (conjunct) or maybe someone will take their ball and go home (opposition). Some aspects create ease (conjunct, sextile) while others create discord (square, Grand Cross) and tension. Aspects are neither good nor bad. They simply show the relationship between planets.

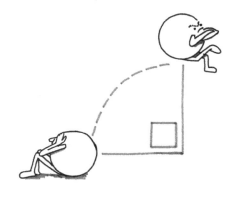

✬ www.shopBigSky.com ✬

Energy Almanac 2020 Edition

Planets

Think of the ten planets as actors from the stories of Roman mythology. Each planet is named after a character in a story, each with its own personality and traits.

SUN

rules the general tone of our being which colors everything else. It rules Leo.

MOON

represents our feelings and emotions, and the receptivity, intuition, imagination and basic feeling nature of a person. It also has an effect on our sense of rhythm and time. It rules Cancer.

MERCURY

is reason, common sense, and that which is rational. It stands for communication, versatility, logical and dynamic order, consideration and evaluation, and the process of learning and skill building. It rules Gemini and Virgo.

VENUS

gives us a sense of beauty, the enjoyment of pleasure, aesthetic awareness, love of harmony, sociability, and taking pleasure in relationships and eroticism. It rules Libra and Taurus.

MARS

represents our energy and drive, our courage, determination, and the freedom of spontaneous impulse. It also describes our readiness for action, the way we go about doing things, as well as aggression. It rules Aries.

JUPITER

represents the search for individual meaning and purpose, optimism, hope, and a sense of justice. It also represents our faith, our basic philosophy for life, wealth, religion, spiritual growth, and expansion. It rules Sagittarius.

SATURN

shows how we experience "reality" and where we meet with resistance and discover our limitations. It represents the conscience, moral convictions, and structure. It also tells us about our powers of endurance and our ability to concentrate. It lends qualities like earnestness, caution, and reserve. It rules Capricorn.

URANUS

stands for intuition and represents originality, independence, and an openness for all that is new, unknown, and unusual. A sort of contrariness is also associated with this planet. It rules Aquarius.

NEPTUNE

gives us the mysterious and supersensory and opens doors to mystical experiences. It speaks to the creative, intuitive, and imaginative. Watch for deception, illusion, and false appearances. Neptune is associated with drug use and many pseudo-realities. It rules Pisces.

PLUTO

describes how we deal with personal and non-personal power. It is how we meet the demonic and magical. Pluto addresses our regenerative powers and our capacity for radical change and rebirth; it is passionate, intense, and global. It rules Scorpio.

The Zodiac

Each zodiac sign carries specific tendencies and traits. The planets are influenced by these qualities as they pass through the sign.

ARIES

MARCH 21–APRIL 19

Fire. Ruled by Mars. Brave, Direct, Fearless, Bold, Independent, Natural born leaders. Aggressive, Pushy, Selfish, Inconsistent.

TAURUS

APRIL 20 – MAY 20

Earth. Ruled by Venus. Steady, Loyal, Tenacious, Trustworthy, Patient. Resistant to change, Stubborn, Materialistic, Indulgent.

GEMINI

MAY 21 – JUNE 20

Air. Ruled by Mercury. Intelligent, Adaptable, Communicative, Agile, Socially connected. Talkative, Superficial, Cunning, Exaggerating.

CANCER

JUNE 21 – JULY 22

Water. Ruled by the Moon. Nurturing, Supportive, Compassionate, Loving, Healing. Dependent, Indirect, Moody, Passive-aggressive, Holds on too long.

LEO

JULY 23 – AUGUST 22

Fire. Ruled by the Sun. Brave, Generous, Charismatic, Fun, Playful, Warm, Protective. Egotistical, Controlling, Drama king/queen, Dominating, Shows off.

VIRGO

AUGUST 23– SEPTEMBER 22

Earth. Ruled by Mercury. Modest, Orderly, Practical, Down-to-earth, Logical, Altruistic, Organized. Obsessive, Perfectionist, Critical, Overly analytical.

LIBRA

SEPTEMBER 23 – OCTOBER 22

Air. Ruled by Venus. Charming, Diplomatic, Polished, Sweet natured, Social. Indecisive, Superficial, Out of balance, Gullible, People pleasing.

SCORPIO

OCTOBER 23 – NOVEMBER 21

Water. Ruled by Mars & Pluto. Passionate, Driven, Perceptive, Determined, Sacrificing, Emotional Depth. Vindictive, Jealous, Paranoid, Destructive, Possessive, Passive-aggressive.

SAGITTARIUS

NOVEMBER 22 – DECEMBER 21

Fire. Ruled by Jupiter. Ambitious, Lucky, Optimistic, Enthusiastic, Open-minded, Moral. Restless, Blunt, Irresponsible, Tactless, Lazy, Overly indulgent.

CAPRICORN

DECEMBER 22 – JANUARY 19

Earth. Ruled by Saturn. Driven, Disciplined, Responsible, Persistent, Business-minded. Pessimistic, Greedy, Cynical, Rigid, Miserly, Ruthless.

AQUARIUS

JANUARY 20 – FEBRUARY 18

Air. Ruled by Saturn & Uranus. Intelligent, Inventive, Humanitarian, Friendly, Reformative. Emotionally detached, Impersonal, Scattered, Non-committal.

PISCES

FEBRUARY 19 – MARCH 20

Water. Ruled by Neptune. Mystical, Intuitive, Compassionate, Romantic, Creative, Sensitive. Escapist, Victim, Codependent, Unrealistic, Submissive, Dependent.

Energy Almanac 2020 Edition

 www.shopBigSky.com

Moon Phases

QUARTERLY QUESTIONS

Each quarter phase of the moon offers you the opportunity to ask a question of yourself for reflection. Use your almanac to mark appropriate dates of Full and New Moons.

The idea of a moon ritual is that you share your intentions and goals with the Universe, God, Higher Power. You're allowing in assistance from all energies on the planet and asking them to participate in your life, and you're doing it under the watchful eye of Grandmother Moon, the wisest crone of them all.

Creating a moon ritual to honor the energy of the moon shouldn't be complicated. You don't need to be able to see the moon or be at the beach to honor this great and powerful energy. You simply need some intentions and a desire for harnessing what is available to you.

Some experts argue the New Moon is for beginning something while others say the New Moon represents the closing of the cycle. Here at The Energy Almanac, it's all about inclusion. We believe the New Moon holds both endings (the closing of the cycle) and beginnings (the start of a new one). With this ritual you are handling both a beginning and an ending, and there is no right or wrong. Your intention to work with moon energy is truly all that is needed.

Make this ritual your own. Add flowers, water, sticks, or money. Subtract what doesn't feel good. This is a guideline for you to use.

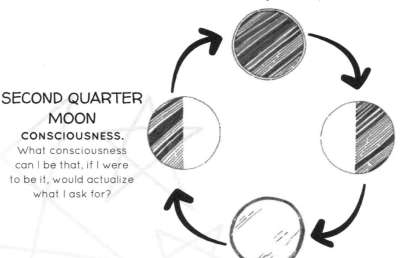

THE NEW MOON
PORTAL OF NEW OPPORTUNITY.
What can I add to my life
that will make my life exceptional?

FIRST QUARTER MOON
ACTION. DIRECTION.
What can I be or do
differently that will
create in a whole
new way?

THE FULL MOON
ILLUMINATION. FRUITION.
What space can I be
for receiving with ease?

SECOND QUARTER MOON
CONSCIOUSNESS.
What consciousness
can I be that, if I were
to be it, would actualize
what I ask for?

Moon Ritual

COLLECT THESE THINGS:

Journal or notebook, pen(s), candle and matches, Moonstone, a bowl or plate, and Sandalwood essential oil.

UNDER A NEW OR FULL MOON, TAKE THESE STEPS:

- Place Moonstone in your pocket to amplify your personal energy. Find a quiet space to sit and write.
- Spend some time journaling about what you'd like closure on in your life. Refer to any area of your life that needs ending. Write it out on a piece of paper. Fold the paper and keep it nearby.
- Spend a second block of time writing on a separate piece of paper about what you'd like to have in place of what you are giving up. The Universe won't tolerate a vacuum, so wherever you remove something, you will replace it with something better. Decide what it is you want and write about it in detail using as much emotion as you can.
- Get as close to the moon as you comfortably can, even if that is just the nearest window. Bring along the candle, matches, gemstone and essential oil.
- Light the candle using your matches and offer the illumination to the Moon. If it's helpful, think of the Moon as a wise old woman who you trust with your whole heart. Tell her, "I light this in your name, in honor of your grace, strength, and power."
- Place a drop of Sandalwood oil on the paper about what you are giving up. You may also place one drop of oil on your brow chakra in center of forehead, one drop on the heart chakra, and one drop on the back of neck at base of skull. Place the paper in the bowl, and use the candle to light the paper on fire. Say, "May the energy of the fire, under the guidance of the moon, transmute and remove this situation from my life." You may also say your own special prayer requesting removal of the issue. Let the paper burn and cool completely before safely disposing of the ashes.
- Place a drop of oil on the paper with your dreams and desires and place it in the bowl. Remove the Moonstone from your pocket and put it on top of the paper. Say a prayer of gratitude. "Thank you for your goodness and grace and the complete fulfillment of my desires. I am wildly open to receiving this."
- Find a comfortable pose. Try the Yogi Squat, Five-pointed Star, or Child Pose, and sit quietly as you contemplate your new goal.
- Leave the bowl out overnight under the energy of the moon.
- In the morning, collect the stone, bowl, and paper. Place the paper in a safe place where you can check on it in a few weeks.
- Lastly, keep your "I" on the prize. Keep your attention and your intention rightly focused on each piece of the puzzle that falls into place. Watch for signs and keep looking for results, thanking your Grandmother Moon all month long.
- Repeat at the next New or Full Moon approximately two weeks later.

Mercury Retrograde

DATES 2020

FEBRUARY 18 – MARCH 9
JUNE 18 – JULY 26
SEPTEMBER 23 – NOVEMBER 20

YES

- EXPECT DELAYS
- FOLLOW UP ON OLD LEADS
- WORK WITH PROJECTS YOU HAVE A HISTORY WITH

NO

- ELECTIVE SURGERIES
- IMPORTANT DECISIONS
- NO VERBAL AGREEMENTS

WHEN MERCURY NAPS NO ONE IS AWAKE TO GOVERN COMMUNICATION

CONFUSION IS NORMAL

Re-

DIRECT
CONNECT
ORGANIZE
VISIT
DESIGN
VIEW

DON'T AGREE TO ANYTHING (YET)

DON'T LAUNCH NEW THINGS

DOUBLE CHECK EVERYTHING!!

WATCH FOR

shifts

Mercury turns retrograde three times each year. This planet rules communication, listening, speaking, contracts, travel plans, negotiating, learning, and technology. Expect those areas of life to feel sluggish or off. Be extremely careful communicating.

✴ www.shopBigSky.com ✴

Energy Almanac 2020 Edition

An Astrological Look at 2020

JANUARY
Restructuring. Rebalancing.
Planning. Boundaries.
Full Moon Lunar Eclipse 1/10
New Moon in Aquarius 1/24

FEBRUARY
Compassion. Intuition.
Details. Facts. Strategy.
Full Moon 2/9
New Moon 2/23

MARCH
Tossing and Turning. Push and Pull.
Introspection. Intentions. Contemplation.
Full Moon 3/9
Spring Equinox 3/19
New Moon 3/24

APRIL
Collective energies. Revealing. Finances.
Manifestation. Strategy.
Full Moon 4/8
New Moon 4/22

MAY
Evolving Minds. Review.
Reflect. Renew.
Full Moon 5/7
New Moon 5/22

JUNE
Rigor. Action.
Concentration. Planning.
Full Moon 6/5
Summer Solstice 6/20
New Moon 6/21

JULY
Restoring Order. Chill.
Rest. Nurture.
Full Moon 7/5
New Moon 7/20

AUGUST
Preparing. Details.
Socialize. Expression.
Full Moon 8/3
New Moon 8/18

SEPTEMBER
Choice. Magic.
Focus. Gratitude.
Full Moon 9/2
New Moon 9/17
Fall Equinox 9/22

OCTOBER
Perspective. Play.
Work. Balance.
Full Moon 10/1
New Moon 10/16
Full Moon 10/31

NOVEMBER
Provocation. Family. Future. Foundation
New Moon 11/15
Full Moon 11/30

DECEMBER
Optimism. Self. Soul Searching.
Seclusion.
New Moon 12/14
Winter Solstice 12/21
Full Moon 12/29

Energy Almanac 2020 Edition

✵ www.shopBigSky.com ✵

About Our Holistic Resources

We are incredibly proud of the group of selected experts in their fields who contributed much time and attention to this publication. Each writer has a complete biography in the back of The Energy Almanac. You are encouraged to reach out to each of them and follow their work more closely, either by social media or via their personal websites, which you will find in the resource section in the back of this book.

ASTROLOGY PERSPECTIVES FOR 2020
BY JANET HICKOX, ASTROLOGER

2020 is likely going to be one wild and (possibly) crazy ride. In the following pages, you're going to read about potentially difficult aspects the planets are making, and hopefully you will also glean tips to navigate the year in holistic and positive ways.

The year 2020 has some incredible astrological transits occurring. Jupiter, Pluto, and Saturn join together in a conjunction in Capricorn not once, but three times next year. This hasn't happened since 1984 BCE (Before Common Era) and even then, the three planets only came together one time. These transits make the year intense, pivotal, and likely a challenging one. Adding to the power of the triple conjunction, both the Moon and Mars will trigger events throughout the year, and in the case of Mars (the God of War) we can expect possible conflict and confrontation as we struggle to evolve in the way we live and work together on this planet.

We can't look into a crystal ball to see what lies ahead for us. What we can do is look back in history and see what happened in the previous triple conjunction (Jupiter, Pluto, Saturn in Capricorn) and predict what themes will likely be active during 2020. What was happening the last time the planets Jupiter, Pluto, and Saturn came together in Capricorn can help us see what might lie ahead.

It was during this part of our history — Ancient Babylonia —that the Code of Hammurabi was created. It was humanity's first draft on laws designed around equality. It began essentially as the edict "An eye for an eye, and a tooth for a tooth." The Code was adopted as a way to level the playing field and make laws applicable to all peoples equally. The Code is still in evidence in the laws we have today. Remarkable, isn't it? What has changed is that we are evolving from the "eye for an eye" mentality and are meant to adopt the "turn the other cheek" philosophy taught by Christ. Sadly, we are not yet there, but the energies of this year are restructuring our laws, beliefs, and values so the pathway to a more evolved idea of equality and the equal application of laws becomes possible. Decades and centuries from now our ancestors will look back on 2020 and say, "That was the year it all changed!"

A Numerological Glimpse Ahead

ANN PERRY, NUMEROLOGIST

What is numerology? Numbers each have a unique energetic vibration. The vibration has a specific meaning. Letters are each represented by a number as well. When you add up the numbers in your name, birthdate, address, or even today's date, and come up with the sum as a single digit, the underlying numerical vibration of that single digit will be at play. You can use numerology to uncover your karmic lessons and debts. You can find out your strengths and weaknesses and even learn about the vibration of your home or business. In their simplest form, each number represents: ➤

1= New beginnings
2= Duality/Decisions
3= Catalyst/Expression
4= Foundation/Focus
5= Movement/Change
6= Nurturing
7= Wisdom/Spirituality
8= Finances/Management
9= Completion

The Energy Almanac invited Ann Perry, professional numerologist, to do the math and reveal the monthly vibrations for 2020. Use the information as an overlay to the astrological information at play this year.

ANN SAYS:

"The new year promises to be a much different energy than that of 2019, which was a 3 universal year, where the focus was on the entertainment industry, music, and the arts. It helped everyone to find their voices, allowing everyone to finally express themselves. You may have noticed many distractions as the 3 created more social demands than usual.

Here comes 2020, where the rubber meets the road!

Add the numbers 2 + 0 + 2 + 0 and the sum total is 4. The year 2020 adds up to a universal year 4, which is about foundation building.

2020 will be a work focused year. This year demands your attention to detail. It will assist us all in creating the solid foundation we all long to have. This is a practical and grounded energy designed to get you well established. The ability to focus is HUGE under the 4 umbrella, so be sure to concentrate on what it is you DO want rather than focusing too long on what you DON'T want. Remember, anything we give our energy and attention to gets bigger. This is especially true for 2020."

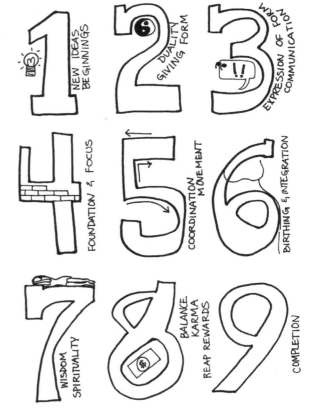

Energy Almanac 2020 Edition

✸ www.shopBigSky.com ✸

Gemstones Wisdom
WITH LISA FONTANELLA, ROCK ENTHUSIAST

Including gemstones in The Energy Almanac will give readers an alternate method for dealing with life's scenarios. You don't ingest them. There is no prescription necessary. Simply find the stone and keep it on your body. At first, carrying a gemstone may feel silly, but once you feel the effects, you may be pleasantly surprised. You can take on the energetic qualities of any gemstone by placing them close to your body for long periods of time. You can wear the stone as a piece of jewelry, such as a ring or pendant, or you can put the stone in your pocket. For best results place the stone directly against your skin. Give the stone a week or so to verify its effectiveness in your situation. If you aren't getting the results you desire, try another stone. All stones mentioned in The Energy Almanac for 2020 are available as a bundle for purchase at our online shop. Please visit: www.shopBigSky.com

More About Essential Oils
WITH STARLA PERICO, HOLISTIC PRACTITIONER AND ESSENTIAL OILS EDUCATOR

Essential Oils are aromatic compounds found in plants and have been used for thousands of years. Oils have extremely effective benefits for physical and emotional well-being. Why are they called *essential oils*? They earned their name because the natural oils within the plant are essential for that plant, tree, or shrub to thrive and survive. When using the oils with the body, they have the same protecting benefits to humans as they do for the plants.

Why would you choose to use essential oils? Science is backing what we already know. Thousands of published studies have shown the physical benefits such as boosting the immune system, calming the nervous system, reducing pain and inflammation, and mood support. Bringing oils into your daily life can help to enhance your overall wellness and balance mood.

When choosing essential oils, be sure to select a 100% pure therapeutic grade oil that has been third party tested for its purity, potency, and efficacy. As essential oils are gaining in popularity, there are a lot of imitation oils on the market. Research the oils you are using if you are going to be using them topically. Depending on the brand of essential oils you choose, you may wish to use a carrier oil for the topical use suggestions provided. Always follow usage instructions on the bottle of essential oil you are using. If uncertain, best practice is to dilute 1-2 drops per 1 teaspoon of carrier oil when applying topically. Oils that can be skin sensitive or warming to the skin will be noted as "topical use dilute with carrier oil" next to the recommended essential oil in this almanac. Citrus oils can be sun sensitive, so it's best to avoid prolonged exposure to sun on the areas where you have applied citrus oils topically. For more advanced usage, you may consult an essential oil reference book.

Note about carrier oils: Fractionated coconut oil is the recommended carrier oil to use for its versatility, shelf stability, and delivery system into the body. Fractionated coconut oil is coconut oil that has had its fatty chain acids removed so it stays in a liquid rather than a solid state. You may also use grape seed, jojoba, avocado, or sunflower oil.

Some of the blend recommendations here in The Energy Almanac can be obtained separately to create your own blend, or for convenience, there are blends already available created synergistically and scientifically for your benefit and ease of use.

Why Yoga
Movement of the Month
BY PENNY ELLIS, YOGA INSTRUCTOR

For thousands of years people have sought the benefits of yoga for relief and healing of physical ailments. While people rarely seek yoga for spiritual enlightenment, after years of a regular practice, that may be the outcome.

When energy is trapped in the body and is not allowed to return to the source, restriction and imbalance can result. With intention, breath, and movement, you assist in releasing restrictions, creating flow and healing within your cells and on all levels.

As health is the free flow of energy, we move toward balancing and aligning our bodies with the universal energy of each month. The movements chosen for The Energy Almanac are just a few of many that will allow for stability with your health. Seeking a yoga teacher in your area will support your growth process. As always, honor your body and consult your physician before beginning a regular yoga practice.

Nourishment Practices
BY HEIDI SYMONDS, THE HEALTHY GODMOTHER

There are big shifts happening in the world and, as empaths and lightworkers, there's a lot of work to do. As *A Course In Miracles* by Helen Schucman says, "The world needs help and God sent you." In order to be of the greatest service for all, you've got to be fully nourished. You have to put your own oxygen mask on first.

✼ www.shopBigSky.com ✼

Think of this section each month like a cozy cafe when you need a little pick me up or a soft place to land. Let these recipes and practices be the guideposts that help you navigate and stay in flow with the seasons and align your chakras. The goal with the way this work is laid out is to help you build and layer your own nourishment practices in a way that supports you at the cellular and SOUL-ular level.

You will find that the focus is on local, seasonal, and sustainable ways of planning and prepping your bio-individual and lifestyle needs with both primary and secondary foods. Secondary foods are the actual foods you eat (food is medicine) and primary foods are all the other ways to nourish yourself for life. The magic, the alchemy if you will, is in trusting yourself, listening to your intuition, and using love as your primary ingredient.

In addition, Heidi Symonds, The Healthy Godmother, has put together a Recipe Page with the seasonal recipes and treats she references each month. They are denoted with an * and can be viewed at TheHealthyGodmother.com/EnergyAlmanac. Be sure to bookmark this page and use the shopping lists, worksheets, and other resources available as part of your weekly/monthly meal planning.

Generative Questions
for Journaling and Self-Coaching
TAM VEILLEUX, QUANTUM LIFESTYLE COACH & CREATIVE

"Why me?" Often times we find ourselves wrapped up in our daily dilemmas and discouragement and end up asking the wrong questions like the one at the beginning of this paragraph. "What is wrong with me? Why does everything seem to go wrong in my life?" Yikes. Those questions are an invitation to disaster.

If you know a little bit about energy or the law of attraction, then you know that what you think about you bring about. Words are creative and build our external lives, so all of those harsh questions you're asking yourself have the potential to create harsh realities. A good pattern interrupt is in order!

What you give your attention to expands, so why not ask something that deserves a beautiful and generative answer? There is a new way of asking questions for your own greater good. At the end of each month's section you'll find a question you can write down and ask repeatedly throughout the month. Then, as time allows and after having asked the question for a bit, journal the generative answer. The questions will help you create results that are growth oriented, forward moving, and inspirational. Through no effort except your attention to the question, your unconscious mind will latch on to your query and create opportunities for you. Your willingness to receive this new information will amplify your results. How does it get any better than this? And what else is possible for you?

The Evolutionary Method
MOTIVATIONS

"To know yourself, you must first sacrifice the illusion that already you do."
—Vironika Tugaleva

In the 2019 edition of The Energy Almanac, we wrote about the 7 human natures, which are taker, spender, earner, saver, investor, lever, giver. You are naturally wired as one of these. It's a lot to take in at once. If you missed that article, please visit **www.project-evolve.com/the-7-natures** for an overview. You'll see a link to a confidential survey to find your nature there as well. This work is not about your personality but rather how your personality expresses itself, as well as how you see and evaluate the external world.

Your nature is only half of what makes you who you are. The other half is your motivation type; it's the engine that informs and drives you to conduct yourself the way you do. To get the best sense of yourself, to know yourself fully, you need to know your nature and your motivation. It may be tricky to identify your motivation type because life absolutely demands we use all of them at different times, however there is one that is your default, your comfort zone. As you read the descriptions below, we'll add some language to help you recognize yourself.

There are only three motivations — Protect, Manage, and Pursue —and they are all vital in this world. Below is an overview with a few stories to illustrate the interplay of nature and motivation. For more, please visit project-evolve.com/case-studies.

PROTECT:

Protectors of any nature subconsciously want to keep what they've got and not lose anything. They behave in ways they think will preserve life as it is because they don't want to backslide. They tend not to take risks and they resist change. This is not a bad thing; it's part of who they are. There are many instances in life when being motivated to protect is healthy and appropriate. Protectors are great at playing defense. In fact, when we brought this curriculum into middle school classes, we had the kids play a modified version of Capture the Flag. They self-sorted by motivation type, and the Protectors naturally became a defensive line.

Protectors look to the past to inform the present, and they are not inclined to look into the future at all. They use language like, "what we've always done in the past," or "we don't want to repeat past mistakes." In a team or committee setting this can seem like they are against any future momentum, and that's not entirely accurate. It's really about an innate drive to preserve their own standing and the position of the organizations, families, and communities about which they care and to which they belong. This can be a position of reason when a group is about to repeat a mistake or take a huge risk. However, the inclination to protect can become a problem.

Protectors, when they don't know about this part of themselves, can turn "protect" into "deny." By protecting what they think they know, they actually deny anything that doesn't fit into that box, and this is usually unconscious. For example, Protectors think twice about sharing information and may not share at all. When Project Evolve was launching, we worked with a business mentor who refused to take our natures survey and demanded to know how we would use his personal information. We don't use personal information; we wanted him to understand our business better. In his perceived need to protect himself and his information, he actually became red with rage and reacted by telling us how our business would fail. Focusing on possible failure is how a Protector attempts to prevent those failures from happening, but his form of protection was not a good fit for our mission. He was unaware of this aspect of himself, and unaware Protectors put up roadblocks to progress and will dismiss ideas that challenge the way they think. While it may be in someone's hardwiring to protect, they don't have to stay in this way of living. To get out of this rut, it's necessary to pivot to a manage mentality and engage with people, ideas, and opportunities that a Protector may otherwise avoid.

Strengths: disaster prevention, pragmatism, caution.

Crisis Response: denial, avoidance, sometimes combative.

Key Questions: Reading this almanac provides insight to what is happening around you, and your motivation type may not be the best skill set to rely on. To help get unstuck, try asking yourself these questions:
- What am I really protecting?
- Do I need to resist this right now?
- Why am I holding back?
- Is holding back the right response?
- Would I be better off if I move in a different direction?

MANAGE:

Managers literally try to keep everything going as it is. Managers are great at managing people, systems, situations, and anything else with multiple facets. In the middle school classes, the kiddos who migrated toward the part of the field where they had to perform multi-part tasks while solving a riddle were the Managers of the group. They weren't interested in capturing the flag, and they didn't want to protect the goal; they were perfectly happy juggling several things at once right in the middle of it all. This is typical of a Manager. They've got their eye on all the parts, pieces, and situations, making choices in an effort to manage life well.

Managers function in the present. They don't look back to the past, and they don't often look up or toward the future. Managers are perfectly suited in organizations with lots of moving parts because they are innately able to focus on many things at once and keep things going. They can manage families, schedules, HR departments, events, and other situations that would cause a Protector or Pursuer to either hide or run away respectively. This is very valuable in a group setting because for a group to function at all it needs people who know how to manage functions and functioning. In fact, Managers are the best ones to run meetings of any kind! Yet despite these attributes, Managers can subconsciously create situations where they overmanage and wrestle with absolutely everything and end up getting nowhere.

Managers are prone to wrestling with their lives to such an extent, that they stay in the same situation for years. If they aren't entirely consumed with wrestling everything all the time, they may allow themselves to desire better relationships, better finances, better businesses, better health, and true self-actualization. However, the future-forward thinking and definitive action personal growth required is simply not in a Manager's wheelhouse. If this goes on long enough, a Manager will end up wrestling with themselves and what they're projecting on to interchangeable people, places, or things. This is truly dysfunctional, and the Manager ends up going nowhere and blaming others. To avoid turning situations or relationships into futile wrestling matches, a Manager can try thinking like a Pursuer and move toward a future where they are managing life better.

Note: *If you are having a hard time determining which is your motivation, you are a Manager. Protectors and Pursuers know immediately, and only Managers wrestle with this!*

Strengths: disaster management, giving directions, multitasking.

Crisis Response: tripping over own feet or freezing/being totally immobilized.

Key Questions: Reading this almanac provides insight to what is happening around you, and your motivation type may not be the best skill set to rely on. To avoid getting stuck, try asking yourself these questions:

• Am I attempting to manage something I can't manage?
• Am I wrestling unsuccessfully?
• Am I more attached to wrestling (negatively) than managing positively?
• Would I be better off if I let go?
• Would I be better off if I move in a different direction?

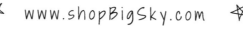

PURSUE:

Pursuers are focused on moving ahead, change, and what comes next in life. Their actions, choices, and behaviors are all aimed at going for what they want. They're not particularly concerned with loss and aren't inclined to simply manage life but instead are motivated to go after whatever is happening next. In the middle school example, the Pursuers were the kids who wanted to capture the other team's flag. They really went for it! Pursuers are future-forward, love all the possibilities, and aren't shy when it comes to change.

Protectors ask, "How did we get here?" Managers ask, "How do we make this function?" Pursuers ask, "What's possible and where can we go from here?" This type of motivation is critical on a team or in an organization that needs to evolve. The Pursuer motivation is necessary for growth, development, and evolution. Pursuers can really go on a tangent pursuing a project, relationship, a diet and exercise plan, or just about anything with great gusto, only to abandon it when something else worth pursuing comes along. They don't know they do this; in fact, they don't know that they take pursuing to an unhealthy extreme because they get so focused on whatever it is they're pursuing.

An unaware person can often become self-consumed, and Pursuers can end up chasing what they think they want and need to a dysfunctional extent. If a Purser is unaware of their motivation, they won't know how to be intentional about their pursuits or to balance their motivation with both protecting and managing. Often Pursuers end up unable to go for what they want and suffer a loss because of it. So, in a way, we can call the opposite of pursue "die." It may be the death of a dream but it's still a loss. Not knowing who they really are can lead to a life of pursuing someone else's dreams or ideals while letting their own fall away, to a life of pursuing things haphazardly, or to a life pursuing nothing at all.

Strengths: being future-forward, going for it, taking action.

Crisis Response: running away/fleeing, pursuing something or someone else.

Key Questions: Reading this almanac provides insight to what is happening around you, and your motivation type may not be the best skill set to rely on. To help get unstuck, try asking yourself these questions:

• What am I really pursuing?
• Do I need to take action right now?
• Am I running from something?
• Is pursuit appropriate in this situation?
• Would I be better off if I pause or move in a different direction?

To know yourself fully, you really do have to set aside what you think you know about yourself. This can be painful as the human ego resists this kind of thinking, but it's worth it to get clear of habitual patterns and beliefs that keep you away from your big, beautiful life. As you go through the year, knowing your nature and motivation will help you apply the tools found in this book most appropriately. You will be able to take care of yourself so you can live a life that honors and supports you. Go now to www.project-evolve.com and discover your nature and motivation.

January

RESTRUCTURING. BALANCE. BOUNDARIES. PLANNING.

DEC 30–JANUARY 5
DO REVIEW FINANCES.
DON'T VIEW STRUGGLE AS NEGATIVE.

JANUARY 6–12
DO CREATE A PLAN FOR WHAT'S NEXT.
DON'T BE REBELLIOUS, BE DETERMINED.

JANUARY 13–19
DO STAY ABOVE THE FRAY OF DISCONTENT.
DON'T FORCE AN ANSWER AS TO WHY.

JANUARY 20–26
DO SEE THINGS WITH A NEW PERSPECTIVE.
DON'T BELIEVE YOUR OLD, LIMITING STORIES.

JANUARY 27–FEBRUARY 2
DO EXPECT SYMBOLIC DREAMS.
DON'T BE SURPRISED BY YOUR OWN SENSE OF KNOWING.

JANUARY 10
FULL MOON ECLIPSE IN CANCER
REBUILDING

JANUARY 24
NEW MOON IN AQUARIUS
INVENTIVE IDEATION

 www.shopBigSky.com

Energy Almanac 2020 Edition

January

······· ✯ ·······

RESTRUCTURING. REBALANCING. PLANNING. BOUNDARIES.

January energies are highly focused across the Capricorn and Cancer axes. This means we are energetically linked to powerful forces along the worldly, business, corporate, and government areas, as well as the more traditional, family-oriented, foundational areas of our lives. The end result is that there are murky waters starting in 2020 as we (we as a civilization, communities, tribes, families) try to rebuild and restructure the world along kinder, gentler, and more compassionate lines. This transition may not happen quickly or easily, but more likely in a step-by-step fashion, and with some bumps along the way. We are definitely moving through transformational times and every one of us are part of it.

DATES TO WATCH:

- **January 2, Mercury conjunct Jupiter.** Prepare for new messages, ideas, or revelations about your next steps for the year.

- **January 3, February 16 Mars in Sagittarius.** In your excitement to grow and expand, be careful not to overdo, overspend, or overextend yourself. The next 6 weeks resonate to adventure and exploration of new ideas and philosophies.

- **January 10, Full Moon Lunar Eclipse.** Potent change is upon us. See January Moons below.

- **January 12, Triple conjunction of Mercury, Saturn, and Pluto.** See below, week 2.

- **January 13, Sun conjuncts Saturn & Pluto.** Possible power struggles, yet the potential to make great strides in something you have been working on. Stay cool, calm, and collected.

- **January 20, Sun moves into Aquarius.** Time to be inventive, see things with new eyes and think outside the box.

- **January 24, New Moon in Aquarius.** See January Moons below.

ASTROLOGY BY THE WEEKS:

WEEK 1: DECEMBER 30, 2019 – JANUARY 5, 2020
The last week of 2019 had planetary movement involving Capricorn along with Mercury who is now in a smooth relationship to Uranus, the awakener.

There is a focus on the financial areas of life first. There is also a connection to laws in this first week of the year. The transits seem to suggest a rebalancing is at play to make laws more fair and equal in their application.

Conservatism is still favored this month. Re-evaluate where you are financially and make changes accordingly.

Shadow: This week confront your tendency to view struggle as negative. When you persevere and use the energy of struggle to create pathways to something new, you end up liberating yourself from old paradigm thinking and behaving.

WEEK 2: JANUARY 6–12, 2020
This week offers a Full Moon Lunar Eclipse in Cancer on the 10th featuring a Sun-Mercury-Saturn-Pluto conjunction opposing the Moon in Cancer and squaring (challenging) Eris, the disruptor, in Aries.

On the world stage, this translates into news about corporations, superpower countries, and government issues. Possible themes are power plays, world trade, climate change, and agriculture/GMOs. Not all the news will be negative. There may indeed be news of advances in these areas. America's presidential election will be in full swing, and some of these topics may show up in the debates and speeches heard around the country.

Personally, you may be grappling with plans for your next steps in life. You may have an urge to stage a rebellion, but before you take rash action, use patience and determination to decide the best course to take next.

On Sunday, January 12, there is an exact triple conjunction of Mercury, Saturn, and Pluto. This is a rare configuration and its meaning is big! There is such a powerful restructuring and rebuilding going on. The three of these planets coming together is like the builder and the architect coming together to build a new house. Mercury delivers the instructions, and Saturn and Pluto destroy/rebuild/rebirth. It's almost poetic based upon the backdrop of everything that has been happening to cause us to evolve and grow in consciousness. Perhaps we see the move from government as an extension of corporations to more community and familial forms? It will be in retrospect that we really see the evidence of what these powerful planets bring us.

Shadow: Greed. When we put profits and earnings above the needs of people and communities, it leads to overall lack and scarcity.

Week 3: January 13–19, 2020

The week starts with a very powerful Sun-Saturn-Pluto conjunction. And, both Venus and Mercury meet up with awakener Uranus this week.

Power struggles and ego clashes could be occurring on the world stage and even in our personal lives. Do your best to stay above that kind of behavior. The high side of this energy is that you can see the changes that are required to be successful on the road ahead.

Our hearts and minds, communication and relationships, all benefit when we elevate our consciousness. Remember that Golden Rule? "Do unto others …" We would do well to remember that this week.

Shadow: Always wanting to know "why" something is the way it is or how something will play out takes away the vital mystery and magic of the Universe. Try instead to adopt awe and wonderment in your life.

Week 4: January 20–26, 2020

This week the Sun moves into Aquarius and meets up in a challenge to Uranus. There is the New Moon in Aquarius (information on the New Moon below), and Mercury and Venus dance with Mars.

The Sun's move into Aquarius reminds us to become more objective about what is going on around us, as there may be more going on than meets the eye. Standing back, we can see things in a new way. Aquarius also resonates with invention and innovation. We want to know how we can re-create ourselves, our work, and our relationships. We're also quite capable of living and behaving in more altruistic and humanitarian ways now as well. The Sun being challenged by Uranus adds a bit of a "dare" to the energies. Uranus says, "I dare you to live by your true self." Will you rise to the occasion?

Shadow: Are you still telling yourself old limiting stories? If so, this is definitely a time to rewrite that story so that you are the hero/heroine of your life's tale.

Week 5: January 27 –February 2, 2020

Neptune in Pisces takes center stage this week as the Moon and Venus in Pisces trigger our more spiritual and intuitive sides.

You may find yourself having highly symbolic dreams and knowing things before they happen. Not to worry. This is how you are designed to live your life. Symbols, dreams, and intuition are all valid ways of knowing. Neptune, Moon, and Venus will remind everyone this week of the more primal ways we have of tapping into consciousness.

January Moons

FULL MOON/LUNAR ECLIPSE IN CANCER @ 20° CANCER | JANUARY 10, AT 2:20 PM ET

MOON MUSINGS:

Physically, the Full Moon occurs when the Sun and Moon are in opposing signs. The Full Moon is a time for releasing, revelation, or completion, and this one is made more powerful by the lunar eclipse. The themes in this Moon cycle are about restructuring, rebuilding, and humanizing government and institutions. As an individual, you may be in a personal rebuilding phase as well. January is always a good time to re-evaluate your life direction, and this month's Lunar Eclipse Full Moon is no exception. Take some time to decide what stays and what goes in your life. Consider applying the word "pruning."

NEW MOON @ 4° AQUARIUS | JANUARY 24, AT 4:43 PM ET

MOON MUSINGS:

The New Moon is a conjunction between the Sun and Moon. They occupy the same degree of the zodiac. The New Moon is a time for new beginnings, starting something fresh, and setting intentions that have power to manifest because you're in alignment with the flow of universal energies. When there is a New Moon in Aquarius, it is time to be inventive and see new solutions to old issues. As Aquarius energy is future-oriented, this is also a great time to employ divination in your life. Get a card reading, an astrology reading (everyone's favorite), or use any other tool that you resonate with.

Aquarius also connects us to friends, groups, and networking. This is a great time to get involved with new people and to see the world from a fresh perspective. Maybe get involved with a humanitarian effort and see how good it feels to be involved in something larger than yourself.

Resources

NUMEROLOGY: 5 UNIVERSAL MONTH IN A 4 UNIVERSAL YEAR

KEY WORDS: BALANCE, PLANNING, BOUNDARIES

The 4 universal year tells us to get focused on a life plan, however, the energy of the 5 universal month says, "But, I don't want to work! I want to play outside." What a contradiction this month produces. On the one hand, you are trying to focus on coloring within the lines, but on the other hand, you really want to break free and experience something outrageously different. This month will be asking you to balance between the need to be disciplined and focused while finding time to experience life outside of the box the 4 often puts you in. This is a great lineup to rethink your plans for the future. The 4 universal year offers you much support to create a solid step by step plan to get you to your goals. But the 5 says, "Hey! Why don't we try something new? We can still be focused even if we invite some new ideas into the mix!" All things in equal measure this month. Maintain some healthy boundaries and try not to be too seduced by the unpredictable energy of the 5. This month is the month of "I didn't see that coming" moments, so plan to be surprised.

GEMSTONE WISDOM: AMBER

While Amber is not technically a gemstone (it's solidified and fossilized tree resin), this beauty is a one-stop-shop for the energies of January. This stabilizing and balancing stone helps to diminish dissention and create a peaceful environment. It's excellent for creating and keeping healthy boundaries. Amber is a great tool in the decision making process and provides the impetus to go after your dreams.

ESSENTIAL OIL APPLICATION:

Setting appropriate intentions from the start of this new year can create new positive patterns of motion and flow. As we enter the restructuring/rebalancing/planning alignment for January, we are laying the pathway for our future endeavors. When the scales of our life are in balance, we become more open to receiving. Since January energies are supportive to new ideas and changes, the oils chosen this month can support keeping you grounded while maintaining a protective shield from outside influences that can otherwise disrupt the balance within.

- **Melaleuca (Tea Tree) -** Apply 1-2 drops to the bottom of each foot. To support healthy boundaries, apply 1 drop to the solar plexus/belly area and 1 drop over center of chest. Tea Tree oil supports you as you are protecting & conserving your physical and emotional energy so that you can be resilient and have positive experiences with those around you. Surround yourself with the protective properties of this oil, and it can act as your energetic "body guard."

- **Grounding Blend -** A blend of Spruce, Ho Wood, Frankincense, Blue Tansy, and Blue Chamomile. Apply 2 drops on the bottom of each foot and 2 drops to the base of spine, near the tailbone. Using this blend of oils offers your whole body the support of being both grounded and connected, promoting the ability to stay focused on the goals and intentions you are creating for yourself.

 www.shopBigSky.com

Energy Almanac 2020 Edition

Chakras supported by these oils: Brow, Throat, Heart, Solar Plexus, Root

POSITIVE AFFIRMATION/INTENTION:
My feet are planted firmly on the ground. I am balanced and centered. I am protected from what does not serve me, and I receive what does serve me.

MOVEMENT OF THE MONTH: WARRIOR II

The energies in Capricorn and Cancer, both earth and water signs, strive for balance with a grounding foundation and loving kindness. This pose, Virabhadrasana II, stabilizes, builds stamina, and opens the sacral chakra. Standing and with an exhale, step or lightly jump your feet 3-4 feet apart. Turn the left foot in and the right foot out. Align the heel of the right foot with the arch of the left foot. Anchor yourself with the mound of the right big toe and the outer edge of the left foot. Inhale and lift your arms to shoulder height. Exhale, as you drop the shoulders down away from your ears.

The tail bone descends toward the floor and the sternum lifts as you bend your right knee, being sure not to extend over the ankle. With intention, connected to your breath, be steady in the pose for up to one minute as you build endurance. Move forward in 2020 with strength and compassion.

NOURISHMENT:

January is usually a time for New Year's Resolutions, new exercise regimens, and restrictive eating/dieting. Refrain from making any extreme changes that usually end up only lasting for a few weeks or months at best. You are being called to "restructure, rebalance, and rebuild" within yourself, your family, and the collective whole. The same applies to your nourishment practices. We are in this for the long haul. Soften into this winter season by incorporating new rituals like starting the day with a Morning Elixir consisting of warm water, green tea, lemon and raw honey. You can add fresh ginger to aid in digestion and/or cayenne pepper to warm. There is plenty of time to build in additional healthy practices to help you reach your goals, but sustainability is the goal.

Astrologically this month taps into and draws on the root and sacral chakras, so adding in lots of root veggies, grounding meats like grass-fed beef, and whole grains will support you in navigating the waters. Speaking of water, did you know that according to Chinese 5 Element Theory, the element of winter is water? More on that next month.

THE HEALTHY GODMOTHER HINT: Winter asks us to pay close attention to the kidneys and bladder. Nourish them with 100% pure cranberry, not from concentrate. It will make you pucker so cut it with coconut water, add a lime and some mint, and it's really quite tasty!

FOODS THAT NOURISH:
- Warming broths and soups
- Root veggies
- Ginger
- Responsibly farmed meats

SEASONAL FOCUS:
- Nourishing the kidneys & bladder
- Sustainability
- Inward focus, quiet, hibernating

CHAKRAS AT PLAY: Root & Sacral

RECIPES:
- Morning Elixir
- Roasted Root Veggies
- Cranberry Flush

JOURNAL THIS:

WHAT CAN I CHOOSE THAT WOULD BRING BALANCE TO MY LIFE?

Love this information? *Get your own private reading or consultation by visiting the writers' personal websites which can be found in the back of The Energy Almanac.*

January Notes

_____

_____

_____

_____

_____

_____

_____

_____

_____

_____

_____

_____

_____

_____

_____

_____

_____

_____

_____

_____

_____

_____

_____

_____

_____

Energy Almanac 2020 Edition

February

COMPASSION. INTUITION. DETAILS. FACTS. STRATEGY.

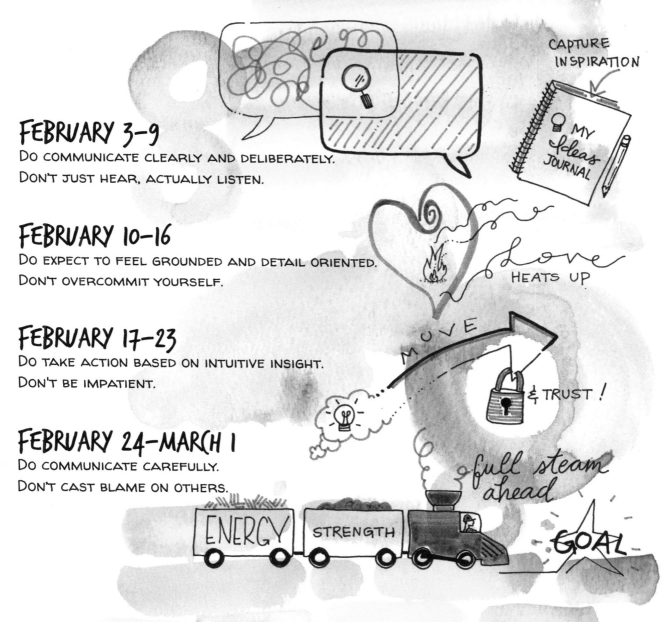

FEBRUARY 3–9
Do communicate clearly and deliberately.
Don't just hear, actually listen.

FEBRUARY 10–16
Do expect to feel grounded and detail oriented.
Don't overcommit yourself.

FEBRUARY 17–23
Do take action based on intuitive insight.
Don't be impatient.

FEBRUARY 24–MARCH 1
Do communicate carefully.
Don't cast blame on others.

FEBRUARY 8
FULL MOON IN LEO
Heart based thinking.

FEBRUARY 23
NEW MOON IN PISCES
Embody compassion for everyone.

Energy Almanac 2020 Edition

✴ www.shopBigSky.com ✴

February

COMPASSION. INTUITION. DETAILS. FACTS. STRATEGY.

February presents us with an interesting blend of planetary transits. Most are producing a more spiritual, compassionate, and intuitive atmosphere on the planet. However, there is that line up of planets in Capricorn leading us through destruction, rebirthing, and restructuring. Even though the dominant energy is softer and more compassionate this month, we are not yet free of the demands of both Saturn and Pluto in Capricorn. Our best bet this month is to be securely anchored in our spiritual identity while being kind and gentle to those who have not yet achieved that level of consciousness.

DATES TO WATCH:

- **February 18-March 9, Mercury retrograde in Aquarius.** Use this time to consider where you want to break free.

- **February 3, Mercury moves into Pisces.** Expect a more compassionate and healing tone in our communication with one another.

- **February 7, Venus moves into Aries.** Venus is wearing her more assertive and bold energy. Watch for conflict in your relationships.

- **February 9, Full Moon in Leo.** See February Moons below.

- **February 16, Mars moves into Capricorn.** Set your goals, make a plan, and work the plan. This is an extremely important move as it has repercussions through the rest of the year.

- **February 16, Mercury turns retrograde from 18 Pisces to 27 Aquarius.** Have your dream and idea journals handy as your inner world may be filled with creative ideas, but don't take action yet.

- **February 18, Sun moves into Pisces.** Compassion, imagination and creativity are at play.

- **February 23, New Moon in Pisces.** See February Moons below.

★ www.shopBigSky.com ★

ASTROLOGY BY THE WEEKS:

WEEK 1: FEBRUARY 3–9, 2020

Mercury and Venus and the Full Moon in Leo take center stage this week. The energy of evolution is pushing us forward and edging us out of our comfort zones.

Mercury moves into Pisces and our minds and communication take on a more imaginative, compassionate and dreamy tone. It might be harder to make yourself understood for the next few weeks, especially with Mercury slowing down to his eventual retrograde later this month. Be sure you are very clear and deliberate in stating what you need to say.

Venus teams up with Saturn, helping our personal and business relationships focus on truth and integrity. This is a great transit to share with your partner what your deepest desires are for a successful relationship.

The Full Moon in Leo reminds us to align with our hearts and to release anything that doesn't feel good to us. (See more in Moon article below.)

Shadow: This week's shadow is about our ability to listen deeply to what others are saying to us. We may "hear" them, but are we really listening? Pay close attention to what the Universe and what people in your life are really telling you. There may be some hidden jewels in what you hear.

WEEK 2: FEBRUARY 10–16, 2020

This week has Moon connections through the signs of Virgo, Libra, and Scorpio.

Expect to feel grounded and detail oriented the first two days of the week. As the Moon transitions into Libra mid-week, our emotions become focused on our relationships. Late in the week (including Valentine's Day), the Moon in Scorpio lights up our passions and our love relationships become more steamy and intense. Good or bad? That depends on how you personally engage your emotions.

Sunday is the focal point of the week's most intense energy as Mars (planet of action) moves into Capricorn where there are already five other planetary bodies for him to interact with. Initially it won't be too difficult, but later in the month things can heat up. Mars will demand us to take action on plans that are based in reality. We will need to focus on actionable steps, not pie-in-the-sky ideals. Mars is the catalyst for change and is in the sign of Capricorn, where there has been a lot of rebuilding, restructuring, and destruction lately. We need to move forward deliberately.

Sunday is also the day that Mercury turns retrograde in Pisces. That means until March 9, we are slowing down, not making any big decisions, and allowing our creative minds to work magic. Get a journal and write down your ideas, but do not take action yet.

Shadow: Watch for half-heartedness. Be careful in what you commit to so you can hold space to complete previous agreements. Look this week at what you are committed to. Are you truly committed and devoted, or are you just half-heartedly in the game? If the answer is that you are only partially engaged, then you must take steps to correct your course or risk burning yourself out.

Week 3: February 17–23, 2020

The pace of the week picks up a bit from last week as the Sun moves into Pisces, Jupiter engages with Neptune in Pisces, Mars and the Sun work with the great awakener Uranus, and we have a New Moon in Pisces.

This week you may feel you are put to work aligning your goals and actions with your creativity, imagination, and intuition. With so much emphasis in the sign of Pisces, we are able to tap into the unseen realm, and if we trust our higher selves, we can do anything. Jupiter sextile Neptune also pushes us to act from our intuition in taking the appropriate steps to our goals.

Mars in Capricorn and the Sun in Pisces both work with Uranus in Taurus this week in helping us see new ways of putting our work out to the world. Since we have been in restructuring and rebuilding phases, we can incorporate the practical, the mystical, and the imaginative in whatever we are doing now. The only thing we have to watch out for is getting caught up in old patterns and behaviors.

The New Moon in Pisces holds some very positive energy for us this week as well. See the Moon article below.

Shadow: Be aware of becoming impatient. This is a week where we have to stay the course to nurture whatever is new in our lives. Trying to make things happen faster will only bring frustration and anger. If you've followed your action steps based on your intuition, then all you have to do is hold space for the magic to happen. Faith and trust will go a long way!

Week 4: February 24–March 1, 2020

This week holds a hodgepodge of energies from the Sun and Mercury sextile Mars, to Mercury conjunct the Sun, and Venus challenging Pluto. The Moon spends most of the week in Aries and Taurus.

We begin the week with the Sun in a favorable aspect to Mars. This is especially powerful as we are still in the light of the New Moon in Pisces. You'll have the energy, fortitude, and strength to carry out the steps you need to take to manifest your intentions. Think of this as an injection of stamina.

Next up is the Mercury retrograde in Pisces conjunct Sun aspect signaling the halfway point of Mercury's retrograde cycle. These two work together to bring in new ideas and a time for mind shifting. Pisces helps you apply intuition in a way that allows you to see the bigger picture.

Venus squares Pluto on the 28th at the same time as the Moon's conjunction to Uranus. Be very careful about how you say what you say to the people you care about; the intended meaning may be misunderstood. Likewise, if someone else says or does something that hurts your feelings, give them a break as transits like these tend to cause us to be unconsciously provocative. This is a short-term transit and will pass quickly enough.

Shadow: When we cast blame or shame on others, it is often a call for us to see ourselves more clearly. Projection occurs when you don't want to confront your own shadows. Processing your emotions and reactions when triggered before lashing out at someone else puts you on the path to conscious evolution.

....

February Moons

FULL MOON @ 20° LEO | FEBRUARY 8/9, AT 2:34 AM ET

MOON MUSINGS:

Physically, the Full Moon occurs when the Sun and Moon are in opposing signs. The Full Moon is a time for releasing, revelation, or completion, and this Full Moon is interesting in that the Moon is holding the weight of all the planets in a bucket pattern. The Moon in this configuration is the handle, while the bulk of the other planets, including the Sun, make up the bucket itself. That means it is your connection to the emotions of love, strength, playfulness, generosity, and joy that will help you release your gifts and talents to the world. When you follow your heart-centered desires, it encourages others to do the same and create a pathway to ultimate bliss. Don't let the conditioning from your parents, society, or culture hold you to ideals, jobs, and relationships that are not true for you. Break free and start living from love.

NEW MOON @ 4° PISCES | FEBRUARY 23, AT 10:32 AM ET

MOON MUSINGS:

The New Moon is a conjunction between the Sun and Moon. They occupy the same degree of the zodiac. The New Moon is a time for new beginnings, starting something fresh, and setting intentions that have power to manifest because you're in alignment with the flow of universal energies.

The New Moon in Pisces is highly creative, imaginative, and intuitive. Here you have the opportunity to create in alignment with your higher self. This degree of the zodiac evokes a connection to ritual and sacredness. If you have never done a ritual manifesting of intentions ceremony with the New Moon before, now is your opportunity. Create a ceremony that honors the co-creative power between you and Spirit. (Revisit the moon ritual in the front section of the almanac.)

The New Moon in Pisces also gives us the opportunity to embody compassion for ourselves and all life on the planet. Feel yourself as part of the whole of the tapestry that is Earth and Universe. Feel how your heart beats in tandem with everything.

....

Resources

NUMEROLOGY: 6 UNIVERSAL MONTH IN A 4 UNIVERSAL YEAR

KEY WORDS: DETAILS, FACTS, STRATEGY

February is a 6 universal month in a 4 universal year. The focus will be on the domestic side of life. This would be a great month to start sketching out the plans. The 6 demands responsibility, especially as it relates to your family. Maybe you are thinking of renovating your home? Maybe it's time to start planning the future for your aging parents? The 6 is also the number of the perfectionist and this can serve you well if you are looking to put the final touches on a plan you've been working on. Your attention to detail will be strong this month. Be careful of being too bossy or nosey this month. The 6 lends itself to gossip as well as the need to be the boss of the planned family reunion. This is also a great month to help your kids make plans for the future.

GEMSTONE WISDOM: JASPER

Just the facts, Ma'am! Jasper collects all your organizational abilities and enhances them if you are organizationally challenged. It encourages keen thinking and gives you the tools needed to see a project through. Jasper will assist you in gathering facts, embracing the details, and creating an imaginative and practical strategy.

ESSENTIAL OIL APPLICATION:

As we focus on compassion, intuition, and strategy this month, this is the perfect time to "hold space". Holding space for others gives them permission to trust their own internal compass and guidance. In doing so, they are free to harness their own power and decision-making processes for their best and highest good. In turn, also be aware of holding space for yourself, and allow the volume on your own intuition to be turned up. Practicing this daily and using the oils recommended can increase compassion for yourself and others.

✧ www.shopBigSky.com ✧

- **Magnolia-** Apply 1-2 drops to the chest/heart area to allow and open your compassionate heart. In addition, you may apply 2 drops to the back of your neck to support the mind/heart connection. This oil allows for feelings of connectedness. This fragrant oil allows you to tap into the part of yourself that yields a heart full of love and invites you to be in alignment with that energy.

- **Clary Sage -** *(avoid if pregnant)* Apply 1 drop between brows (center of forehead). No matter where you are at with your intuitive abilities, using Clary Sage to enhance those abilities this month could prove to be beneficial. When we spend too much time "in our head", it quiets our intuition. Intuition is an innate gift that we are all born with. Using Clary Sage can clear the cobwebs that may be blocking your own intuitive guidance .

Chakras supported by these oils: Brow, Heart

POSITIVE AFFIRMATION/INTENTION:
I am connected to others in ways that support my highest good and theirs. I trust the wisdom within me will guide me.

MOVEMENT OF THE MONTH: WARRIOR 1

Virabhadrasana (Warrior I) is a powerful posture. Think of removing obstacles with the strength of a warrior. During the month of February, the energy is pushing us forward and edging us out of our comfort zones. Stand in Mountain Pose. With an exhale, step or lightly jump your left leg back. Turn the left foot in and the right foot out. Plug into the mound of the right big toe and the outer edge of your left foot to anchor to the earth. Inhale and bring arms overhead. As you exhale, lunge into a right angle with the front leg leading with your hips. Be sure your knee does not extend beyond your ankle. With both hips facing forward, root down in your feet as you extend your arms overhead, keeping them in line with your ears. Your shoulders drop down away from the ears. Hands may be palms together or apart overhead. Focus on your breath, taking 3- 5 breaths, anchoring in the pose as you allow yourself to drop deeper into the earth as you simultaneously ascend energetically toward the heavens. Lift your ribcage away from your pelvis. Keep your head in a neutral position, gazing forward. The seasoned practitioner may tilt their head back and look up at your thumbs, taking the pose a bit deeper.

Energy Almanac 2020 Edition

NOURISHMENT:

Remember, we are focusing on sustainability. We are in this for the long haul. Water (element of winter) is life force. It's often the fastest way to feel better when fatigued, hungry, or moody. If you're going to build a strong nourishment practice to support the work that's being presented, you need to stay hydrated. Be sure to drink half your weight in ounces daily.

Another piece of sustainability is how much you're putting on your plate... and how many plates you're spinning at one time. We think we have to do it all, but in trying to do it all, we can crash and burn. It's important to be mindful of what goes on your plate. Choose foods (people and activities too) that are wholesome, made with love, and responsibly grown. Heart-centered living starts with nourishing yourself with the most sacred ingredients. When possible, buy local and organic and avoid highly processed foods. Soups and broths are super comforting this time of year, and be sure to incorporate lots of purple and blue foods like my Crown Chakra Shepard's Pie, as well as steamed or sautéed greens to support the chakras at play!

THE HEALTHY GODMOTHER HINT: Making chocolate dipped strawberries for yourself or a special someone you want to love on? Add a teaspoon/tablespoon of coconut oil (depending on how many yummies you're making) to your melted dark chocolate to keep it wrapped around the strawberry (organic if possible because berries are on the Dirty Dozen list) rather than have it break up in your lap! The idea is to eat the chocolate and the berry TOGETHER ... am I right?

FOODS THAT NOURISH:

- Soups, broths
- Roasted veggies
- Comfort foods

SEASONAL FOCUS:

- Kidneys and bladder
- Hydration

CHAKRAS AT PLAY: Heart, Third Eye, Crown

RECIPES:

- Infused Water Guide
- Dirty Dozen/Clean Fifteen
- Crown Chakra Shepard's Pie

JOURNAL THIS:

WHAT IS THE BENEFIT OF HEART—CENTERED LIVING?

HOW CAN I BE THE MOST COMPASSIONATE ME POSSIBLE?

Love this information? Get your own private reading or consultation by visiting the writers' personal websites which can be found in the back of The Energy Almanac.

February Notes

March

TOSSING AND TURNING. INTROSPECTION. INTENTIONS. CONTEMPLATION.

POSSIBLE TECHNOLOGY ISSUES

CLEAN UP!

MARCH 2-8

DO PRACTICE SELF-CARE AND DO BACK UP YOUR DIGITAL WORLD.
DON'T BE TRAPPED IN RIGID THINKING.

my Plan: A B C + imagination = yes

I'LL HAVE THIS...

MARCH 9-15

DO CLEAN YOUR SPACE.
DON'T STAY STUCK FEELING MELANCHOLY.

DREAM Big

CELEBRATE

SPRING'S ARRIVAL WITH GOAL SETTING

MARCH 16-22

DO SET NEW, BIG GOALS.
DON'T ALLOW CONFLICT. SLOW DOWN AND BREATHE.

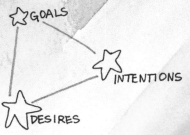

☆ GOALS

☆ INTENTIONS

MARCH 23-29

DO SET POWERFUL NEW INTENTIONS.
DON'T BE REACTIVE.

☆ DESIRES

MARCH 9

FULL MOON SUPERMOON IN VIRGO
A TIME OF PURIFICATION.

MARCH 24

NEW MOON IN ARIES
MAKE A CHOICE TO RELEASE OLD DIALOG.

Energy Almanac 2020 Edition

 www.shopBigSky.com

TOSSING AND TURNING. INTROSPECTION. INTENTIONS. CONTEMPLATION.

March provides us with an interesting array of energies. You are familiar with the "March comes in like a lion and goes out like a lamb" saying, but astrologically speaking, this month is more like lamb, lion, lion, lamb, as we experience a bit of tossing and turning. You may not feel like the earth is solid beneath your feet this month. You may feel more like pizza dough – tossed up in the air, reshaped, then tossed up again. The net result is a positive force for change in the world and within each one of us. Try to stay in your center as much as possible this month.

DATES TO WATCH:

- **March 4, Mercury retrogrades into Aquarius.** Returns us to more mind-oriented considerations. Contemplate freedom and where your brilliance lies.

- **March 4, Venus into Taurus.** Delight in the sensual, spend money wisely, and beautify your home, office, or your own body.

- **March 9, Mercury Direct + Full Moon in Virgo.** Don't begin anything new until after the retrograde ends. See March Moons below.

- **March 16, Mercury into Pisces.** Mercury triggers our imagination, sensitivity, compassion. Confront your escapist tendencies.

- **March 19, Sun into Aries/Spring/Autumn Equinox.** A time for new beginnings and boldly moving forward. The beginning of the astrological new year.

- **March 21, Saturn into Aquarius.** Building toward innovative and inventive structures. Humanitarian focus based on community.

- **March 24, New Moon in Aries.** See March Moons below.

- **March 30, Mars into Aquarius.** Prepare to move forward in new and unique ways.

ASTROLOGY BY THE WEEKS:

WEEK 1: MARCH 2–8, 2020

The week begins with the Moon in Gemini. Venus challenges Saturn and conjuncts Uranus this week. The Sun conjuncts Neptune in Pisces.

You can expect a fairly quiet start to the month of March with most of the planetary movements bringing up positive energies. The Moon moves through Gemini, Cancer, and Leo. On Monday, we face the "crisis of action" phase of the New Moon cycle started at the end of February. This is when you face the outer world resistance to creating or manifesting your intentions. At this point in the cycle, it is important not to give up on yourself and to keep following the outer world cues that lead you forward.

On Wednesday, Mercury retrogrades back into Aquarius. Be prepared for possible technology challenges for the next week. Backup your computer and other devices in case of problems. Venus also moves into Taurus today, and that sets us up for some wonderfully sensual, comfortable, and loving experiences. Take some time for self-care, bolster your relationships through nurturing, and maybe remodel or redecorate your home. When Venus is in Taurus it is also a great time to update your look – hair, make up, clothing, and style.

Sunday may be an interesting day as the Sun conjuncts Neptune and Venus conjuncts Uranus. Expect surprises. This won't be a great day to make decisions as you may be more interested in spiritual pursuits or in escapist activities.

Shadow: Confusion and rigid thinking. This week is one to practice being open-minded and exploring new ideas and concepts. When you hold yourself fast to old paradigm thinking, you hold in place conflict and separation. It's time to step out of "stinkin' thinkin'", try on new ideas, and see new ways of living and working together.

WEEK 2: MARCH 9–15, 2020

The Moon moves through Virgo, Libra, Scorpio and Sagittarius this week. The Sun and Jupiter work together to further our goals, and Mars meets up with Neptune to remind us of our spiritual heritage. Lastly, the Sun meets up with Pluto as a way to empower our personal and collective transformation.

We begin this week with the Moon in Virgo which favors grounded, practical, and organized action. Plan your week ahead and see to the details. Virgo favors clean environments with minimal clutter. Clean your space this week!

By mid-week, the Moon is in Libra focusing on relationships and urging us to the three C's – cooperation, co-creation, and collaboration. The Moon in Libra loves to harmonize and balance. Wednesday brings the Sun and Jupiter into a positive alliance that blends our imagination with practical steps to achieving our goals. It's possible that teamwork becomes the pathway for getting where we want to go in our lives.

Thursday is a bit of an irritating day as the Moon challenges Saturn and opposes Uranus and Venus. Moon-Saturn connections tend to cause us to withdraw to our inner world. You may feel less conversational and social. This is sometimes interpreted as depression or melancholy. Not to worry though. The Moon moves quickly and you will feel better by Friday. The Moon opposing both Uranus and Venus can bring unexpected financial or relationship challenges. Tempers and feelings may be running a little hot.

Shadow: The shadow of not confronting your shadow. We have a choice when it comes to fear and that is to confront it and transmute it or turn away from the shadow and keep fear empowered. This week do not be afraid to look deeply within and transmute whatever it is that holds you back from living your most wonderful life.

WEEK 3: MARCH 16–22, 2020

Mercury moves forward into Pisces this week, and the Sun begins the astrological new year with its move into Aries. Mars and Jupiter meet up in Capricorn, and then Saturn moves into Aquarius for the first time in almost 30 years! The week ends with Mars' conjunction to Pluto.

It's a good time to finish something, spend time in goal setting, make a list of things to do, or meditate. Get down to business later in the week. You might be faced with the inner shift required to continue manifesting your intentions set at the New Moon. Release judgments, patterns, grievances, and any victim energy you are holding on to.

Mercury moves into Pisces as well on Monday. Your mind and communication become more emotional, compassionate, and imaginative. You may be more inclined to follow your inner guidance and intuition. You are encouraged to go slowly and check and recheck everything you say or do before you say or do it.

Thursday is the Spring/Fall Equinox, and so begins the astrological new year. The Sun is in a sweet flow with Saturn, so dare to dream big and set goals that will expand your genius for the coming year. The Spring/Fall Equinox is an optimal time for goal setting. It aligns you with the flow of energy in the solar system.

Mars conjunct Jupiter heralds a new two year cycle of growth and expansion. They come together in the sign of Capricorn to help us define how we express our authority and authenticity in the world. We become more focused on sustainable growth. Two days later, Mars conjuncts Pluto. This spells excitement, possible danger, and upheaval (change, revolution, evolution). The world, and you as an individual, are transforming. The quest here is to be able to consciously choose what our values are and then to live by demonstrating them in the world.

Saturday (meaning Saturn's Day) the planet Saturn moves out of Capricorn and into Aquarius for a short three month stay, giving you a taste of what your new lessons will be when he moves in for his longer visit later this year. Saturn lessons in Aquarius will be about humanitarianism, bringing more fairness to all beings, and how to live in the great "brotherhood of man" consciousness. Be prepared for significant shifts in how we work with one another.

Shadow: Conflict and reaction are the two shadows we are dealing with this week. In reality we could say that how you react to conflict is what you are learning. When in reactive mode, you lose peace of mind and become blind to alternate solutions. If you give yourself a chance to breathe before you react, you can choose how to respond. This is called being response-able.

Week 4: March 23–29, 2020

A quieter week prevails! The high point of the week is the New Moon in Aries and Venus in a lovely flow with Jupiter and Pluto.

The New Moon in Aries gives everyone another shot at beginnings. Think of the New Moon in Aries as the most powerful intention-setting Moon of the astrological year. You have initiative, drive, and ambition to make change and move forward with your work and lives. See March Moons below.

There are a few bumps this week with challenges by the Moon to Jupiter, Pluto, Mars, Saturn and Uranus. If you're feeling emotional, it is all a part of the energy of this week. Breathe and give yourself space before you react to what is going on in your world. This won't last for very long, and later in the week Venus comes along to smooth out some of the rough spots. Love (Venus energy) is always the answer.

Shadow: Emotional reactivity is the shadow for this week which builds upon last week's shadow of conflict. This week's energy has been emotional, yet not an excuse to overreact to the world around you. To do so leads to being victims or to victimizing others by your emotions. Feel your emotions but don't use them as an excuse to behave badly.

....

March Moons

FULL MOON/SUPERMOON @ 20° VIRGO | MARCH 9, AT 1:48 PM ET

MOON MUSINGS:

The Full Moon in Virgo this month opposes Neptune in Pisces, and it is a Supermoon, meaning it has more effect on us as it is closer to the earth than usual. Right now, you may be extraordinarily sensitive to your environment, to other people in your life, and to anything you take into your body. Surround yourself now with gentleness and compassion. If the world seems harsh, you may need to move more inward through meditation, prayer, or yoga for balance.

A Full Moon in relation to Neptune can also cause strange dreams, moods, and feelings to come up to the surface – from the deep of our subconscious to the light of our waking day. Don't be alarmed, but rather, look for the symbolic meaning for you. What is your subconscious mind trying to communicate to you?

✴ www.shopBigSky.com ✴

Avoid the use of drugs or alcohol to excess now as your body is also super sensitive. Don't be surprised if you have allergic reactions to things in your environment. All is well. We are simply in a time of purification and returning ourselves to a more holistic and organic way of living.

NEW MOON @ 4° ARIES | MARCH 24, AT 5:29 AM ET

MOON MUSINGS:

Are you ready to release yourself from the wounds and shadows that have held you back in life? If so, then this is your time to release yourself from the chains that bind and move forward fearlessly into the possible unknown.

A New Moon allows you to set powerful intentions for manifesting your dreams, goals, and wishes. This New Moon is conjunct both Chiron (our wound) and the Black Moon Lilith (your shadow or fear) and this means you can push past all the old dialog, the old patterns, and the old beliefs you have held about yourself.

On the other hand, the wounds and fears are right in your face now, and it is up to you to choose what you do with it all. Do you want to keep expressing the same old same old? Or do you want to release yourself and be free? Now is the time to choose.

Above all, keep your mind on what you want to create.

....

Resources

NUMEROLOGY: 7 UNIVERSAL MONTH IN A 4 UNIVERSAL YEAR

KEY WORDS: INTROSPECTION, INTENTIONS, CONTEMPLATION

After last month's demands from family, this month you get to curl up in your cave. The 7 universal month asks us to go within. It asks us to take some time out to figure out what our next step is. What do you want? Where do you want to be two years from now? How do you plan on getting there? There it is! The 4 universal year is a planning year, so this is an excellent lineup for future planning. Don't make too many social plans this month because, honestly, you won't feel like playing. You will need lots of time alone as you ponder your next move. Consider this your required stint in the time-out-chair. It's a month of quiet reflection with a healthy dose of introspection. Even though the 4 demands that you make progress with your plans, the 7 universal month says, "I'm thinking right now. I'll get back to you."

✬ www.shopBigSky.com ✬

GEMSTONE WISDOM: LABRADORITE

Ahhh. This is the calming energy of Labradorite. Once your overactive "monkey mind" chills out, it's time to sit back and be open to new possibilities. Labradorite supports contemplation and encourages you to ask yourself what it is that you truly want. Be bold. Have you heard the saying "Say yes when it seems crazy"? Is there something crazy you want to try? Set your intention, embrace wonderful new ideas, and be receptive to opportunities that come your way.

ESSENTIAL OIL APPLICATION:

Hello Mercury Retrograde! The compassion you cultivated last month can serve you with the energies at play this month. We are sitting with introspection/intentions/contemplative themes in March. Mercury Retrograde is a time of re-evaluating what is important to you and discerning what isn't. Nurturing harmony at this time utilizing the selected oils can prove to be rewarding. Especially if you are someone that tends to be more emotionally charged during Mercury retrograde, using the following oils can ease the conflicted feelings that may present themselves during this time.

- **Cypress-** Apply 1-2 drops on any area of the body that you feel may need assistance with movement and flow. Cypress is a powerful mover of stuck energy. Emotions can get trapped within the body. Cypress can free up those emotions to allow them to be processed and shifted, allowing you to release those dense areas within the body that may be holding you up from moving forward.

- **Ginger -** (topical use carrier oil) Apply 2 drops to the bottom of each foot. Place 1-2 drops into a diffuser. Ginger offers empowerment to those who may be feeling powerless, stuck or in fear. When circumstance feel outside of your control, used ginger to encourage personal responsibility and acceptance. This can enable you to take your power back rather than feeling powerless to others, circumstances or events.

Chakras supported by these oils: Throat, Solar Plexus, Root

POSITIVE AFFIRMATION/INTENTION:
*I am supported with my positive intentions. I invite harmony
into every moment of my day.*

MOVEMENT OF THE MONTH: COBRA POSE

To assist in aligning with the energy of March, you can practice Cobra Pose, Sanskrit, for increasing energy, introspection, and awakening your spiritual insight.

Lying prone on the floor with tops of the feet on the floor, all ten toes touching including your pinky toes, place your hands under the shoulders. Spread your fingers apart evenly, and move your pubis bone to earth to provide an anchor. Draw your shoulders down and away from the ears, moving elbows toward each other. Inhale, lifting through the back of your head, lift chest and abdomen. Keep your elbows tucked to your side ribs, extend through your front body as your feet are anchored to the floor. Slowly exhale and release to the floor. Rest for a moment with the head to one side or forehead on the floor. This is a beginner backbend and should be done with the breath for several repetitions. It is not meant to be held for many breaths. It is the repetitions that create the heat of transformation and introspection. Remember to pause after each repetition. Feel the heat of the movement and the flow of energy it creates.

NOURISHMENT:

As you nourish your way through the bumpy transition from winter to spring, there's also a call to stand in the messy (and often muddy) middle. Stay away from all-or-nothing and black-or-white ways of being in your life and nourishment practices.

The days of "on the wagon/off the wagon" are over. There's too much work to do to be caught in the cycle of "all in" with perfectionism running the show. It's not sustainable. Use the 80/20 rule: 80% of the time, focus on making food and lifestyle choices that you know are the most loving and nourishing for how you want to feel and show up in the world; 20% of the time, you can make choices that fill you up in other ways or provide comfort from all of the tossing and turning of this moon cycle. Please note, some seasons require periods of 90/10 and others call for sliding down to 70/30 or even 60/40… but you are always on the continuum someplace and wherever you are is perfect. Zero judgment. As you build your nourishment plan into a daily spiritual practice, ask yourself, "Based on what's on my plate this day/week/month/season, how do I want to feel?" Listen for the answer and adjust accordingly.

THE HEALTHY GODMOTHER HINT: As you put your fear aside and step deeper into transmuting the things that are holding you back and find yourself needing a little something to dull the edges, fill 2 halved and pitted medjool dates with peanut butter and top with 2 dark chocolate chips on each one. Fast. Easy. Scratches the itch and doesn't leave a whole batch of cookies calling to you all night.

FOODS THAT NOURISH:

- Soups & broths: Continue to nourish
- Beets, carrots, & sweet potato
- Seeds (of intentions)

SEASONAL FOCUS:

- Winter to Spring
- Nourishing liver & gallbladder

CHAKRAS AT PLAY: Root, Sacral

RECIPES:

- Chia Pudding
- Nourish Yourself Breakfast Bowl
- Salted Caramel Chocolate Mousse

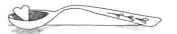

JOURNAL THIS:

WHAT POINT OF VIEW CAN I CHOOSE THAT CREATES AND GENERATES A MORE GROUNDED ME? WHAT CONTRIBUTION CAN INTROSPECTION BE TO MY LIFE?

Love this information? Get your own private reading or consultation by visiting the writers' personal websites which can be found in the back of The Energy Almanac.

March Notes

April

COLLECTIVE ENERGIES. REVEALING. FINANCES. MANIFESTATION. STRATEGY.

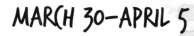

MARCH 30–APRIL 5

DO REFOCUS YOUR TIME.
DON'T HARBOR DYSFUNCTIONAL BELIEFS.

APRIL 6–12

DO LOOK FOR CREATIVE LIFE SOLUTIONS.
DONT STRIVE TO CONTROL SITUATIONS.

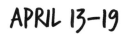

APRIL 13–19

DO EXPECT TO FEEL MORE SOMBER.
DON'T RESIST THE CHANGES THAT ARE HAPPENING.

APRIL 20–26

DO WORK TOWARD RELEASING OLD BELIEFS.
DON'T BE NARROW-MINDED.

go with the flow

SEE FROM A NEW PERSPECTIVE

APRIL 27–MAY 3

DO BE PREPARED FOR SURPRISES.
DON'T BE AGGRESSIVE, MOVE TOWARDS LOVE.

APRIL 7
FULL MOON SUPERMOON IN ARIES
CREATING HARMONIOUS RELATIONSHIPS.

APRIL 22
NEW MOON IN TAURUS
SEEK NEW WAYS TO SOLVE OLD PROBLEMS.

Energy Almanac 2020 Edition

 www.shopBigSky.com

April

COLLECTIVE ENERGIES. REVEALING.
ADJUSTING. FINANCES. MANIFESTATION

January brought us the beginning of a new era, and in April the next steps of the journey are being revealed to us. Most of the month you can be concerned with collective and generational energies that will reshape our society, culture, businesses, major institutions and values over the next few years. As individuals we are also a part of these big cycles and have a role to play in determining next steps. Living in alignment with the highest principles and values possible helps all of humanity. You hold the key to the successful transformation happening on planet Earth.

DATES TO WATCH:

- **March 30, Saturn into Aquarius.** (as a reminder from last month)

- **March 31, Mars conjunct Saturn.** Channel any anger or frustration into work today to avoid conflict with others.

- **April 3, Venus into Gemini.** Venus in her Gemini garb is fun and flirtatious, albeit a bit non-committal.

- **April 5, Jupiter-Pluto conjunction at 24 Capricorn.** Focus on blending the best of your traditions with the highest potential of how you can work together now.

- **April 7, Full Moon in Libra.** Relationships being rebalanced to ensure harmony.

- **April 10, Mercury into Aries.** The pace of life speeds up when Mercury moves into Aries. Be prepared for more work, more communication, and a quick thinking and acting mind.

- **April 19, Sun into Taurus.** Focus on manifesting, being on solid footing in your relationships, work, and your financial health.

- **April 22, New Moon in Taurus.** The time is now to set powerful intentions that have greater manifesting power. Be careful that your thoughts are on what you desire and not on what you don't want.

- **April 25, Pluto turns retrograde.** The planet of power and transformation moves us to change on the inner planes for the next 5 months.

- **April 27, Mercury into Taurus.** When the messenger planet moves into Taurus, we become more focused on the practical. Our speech and mind works at a more deliberate and slower pace.

✷ www.shopBigSky.com ✷

ASTROLOGY BY THE WEEKS:

WEEK 1: MARCH 30 – APRIL 5, 2020

Power week ahead! Mars conjuncts Saturn, Mercury conjuncts Neptune, and perhaps the most impactful event this week, Jupiter conjuncts Pluto in Capricorn, triggering the next steps in our societal and cultural transformation.

Early in the week, things will get going. Communication is present as are your emotions. By mid-week, emotional triggers abound. Process those before communicating, or you risk being misunderstood.

Biggest news of this week is Saturday's Jupiter conjunct Pluto. Jupiter only conjuncts Pluto once every 13 years, so it is unique. This conjunction is part of an ongoing Jupiter-Saturn-Pluto conjunction that hasn't happened since 1894 BCE (Before Common Era). This is an earth-shaking event. Be aware of the societal, cultural, political, institutional, and economic changes that are occurring.

Jupiter conjunct Pluto is likely to cause you to re-evaluate your life direction and refocus where you are spending your time. Consider how you show up in the world.

Shadow: Dysfunctional beliefs and emotional immaturity make up the shadow for this week. You are presented with a perfect opportunity to change the beliefs, thoughts, and emotional states that have held you in victim energy. Use your emotions as a barometer of what needs to change or shift.

WEEK 2: APRIL 6–12, 2020

The Moon trines all the planets in Capricorn, then squares them, then sextiles them. Translation: prepare for many emotional ups and downs.

The most impactful day this week is likely Tuesday, when Mars (warrior) challenges Uranus (the awakener) at the Full Moon in Libra. You may have a tough time maintaining harmony and diplomacy.

Mercury's voice in Pisces cuts through at times this week. Pisces reminds us about compassion, being imaginative, and finding creative solutions to our problems. On Friday, however, Mercury moves into Aries and even he will lose patience with the cacophony. Try hard to maintain your equilibrium and inner peace this week.

Shadow: Control. You may feel like you are unable to control anything in your environment. This triggers us to try to exert more control on situations, people, and events going on around us. Learn to go with the flow.

WEEK 3: APRIL 13–19, 2020

The Sun in late degrees of Aries challenges both Pluto and Jupiter this week, shining more light on what is happening on the world stage. We may see or experience ego conflicts and power struggles between people.

The Moon, moving through Capricorn early this week, conjuncts Pluto, Jupiter, and Mars. You may be feeling emotional overload from last week, and now this week you could find yourself refraining from your emotions. You may feel more sober or melancholic. Don't be worried. This is the natural ebb and flow of emotional energy.

Later in the week, the Sun shifts into Taurus, and we move into the "master manifesting" time of year. Remember that what you are thinking about, focusing on, and attaching emotion to is manifesting very quickly now.

Shadow: Chaos, resisting change, and transformation. This third week of the month is a combination of all the shadows for the month. Society and humanity are undergoing a huge shift, and that puts many people on edge and fearful. When fearful, you may tend to dig your heels in and resist, which can then turn into chaos. Choose peace this week. Release attachment to what is happening around you.

WEEK 4: APRIL 20–26, 2020

Challenges abound this week as the Moon, Sun, and Mercury take turns squaring planets in Capricorn (Saturn, Pluto, Jupiter), and the Sun comes to its annual conjunction with Uranus. You may be surprised, shocked, or excited by the events around us.

One by one, the Moon will challenge the planets in Capricorn. We are in the midst of restructuring, rebuilding, and finding our personal inner authority. You must have a plan, work the plan, and lay a solid foundation first.

The New Moon in Taurus occurs on Earth Day and reminds us that the most sustainable foundations are built resourcefully and by being good stewards of the earth. See New Moon section below.

Mercury in late Aries also challenges Pluto and Jupiter this week. Mercury as the communicator and thought guru wants your thinking to be clear, concise, and simple. You may have to wade through your mind to release anything getting in the way of your evolution.

The Sun conjunct Uranus in Taurus gives us insight and genius, particularly as it relates to our finances and values. Life may open up surprising new pathways for you now, especially as we are still in the window of the Taurus New Moon.

Shadow: Fear over love. We become narrow-minded and blinded when we choose to see things from a fearful perspective. This week offers you opportunities to see from a higher perspective; see from the heart instead of the mind.

✢ www.shopBigSky.com ✢

Week 5: April 27 – May 3, 2020

The month ends with a couple of transits this week that may create some stress: Mercury square Saturn and Mercury conjunct Uranus.

While the Moon does her usual dance through the signs this week, there are a couple of days where the emotional energy may be difficult. On Wednesday, the Moon in Cancer opposes the planets in Capricorn - Pluto, Jupiter, and Saturn. On Thursday, the Moon squares Mercury, Uranus, and the Sun. Our emotions are up and down, moody and unpredictable. Don't overreact or be reactionary. Others around you may be difficult; have compassion. They may not understand what is going on.

Mercury in Taurus can help us keep our minds on simplicity and practical topics. However, the Mercury/Uranus connection can make for some surprises this week! Possibilities run the gamut from epiphany to revolution. Be prepared for anything, stay calm, and focus on what is possible.

Shadow: Competitiveness and aggression are the shadows this week. Both of these energies are based in the fear of not having or being enough. Move toward love and seek positive expressions.

....

April Moons

FULL MOON/SUPERMOON @ 19° ARIES | APRIL 7, AT 10:35 PM ET

MOON MUSINGS:
There is so much potential in this Full Moon in Libra. The Moon holds the handle of a bucket pattern, which sets our priority on creating and building harmonious, mature relationships. This is also a Supermoon, which means that the Moon is very close to the Earth (at least within 90% of the closest she ever comes to Earth), and the tides of our emotions are very high. The high side is that we can be diplomatic, tactful, and cooperative. At the lowest, we may still be grappling with divisive polarity. What's clear in the Full Moon is its power to allow us to release and complete the old in order to embrace the new.

Ask yourself what is worthwhile and supportive in your life and in the world and build on that. Let go of anything else that doesn't support harmony or win-win situations.

✳ www.shopBigSky.com ✳

NEW MOON @ 3° TAURUS | APRIL 22, AT 10:27 PM ET

MOON MUSINGS:

Like the Full Moon earlier in the month, the New Moon is powerful and packs quite a punch. The energy of the New Moon is always about creating something new, and this month the New Moon in Taurus is conjunct Uranus, thrusting change upon us if we don't voluntarily or consciously move in that direction. The Moon and Sun are also challenging or challenged by Jupiter, Saturn, and Pluto. This trio of planets are ultimately responsible for the cultural, societal, and institutional upheavals we have been going through. This moon holds the potential for you to connect to new ways of solving old problems, both personally and collectively. Don't become alarmed by the likely dramas playing out in the world around you as everything is literally happening in the right way, at the right time, and in our highest and best interest. Keep the faith, trust in a higher power, and keep shining your light.

....

Resources

NUMEROLOGY: 8 UNIVERSAL MONTH IN A 4 UNIVERSAL YEAR

KEY WORDS: FINANCES, MANIFESTATION, STRATEGY

Wowzers! This lineup doesn't happen too often, so take advantage of its vibration. The 4 universal year says this is a time to plan and the 8 universal month says we need to create a financial plan! Make sure you make an appointment with a financial advisor this month. Nothing says manifestation like the number 8 does. The 8 is also a reminder to take back your power anywhere you may have previously surrendered it. The energy of the 8 is not just about your money. It's also about your personal power too. What is your plan to start taking your power back? Ask yourself, "What have I been doing to create my current reality? Ask yourself what you have been doing to create your current situation. Where have you been treated with disrespect or like a doormat? What did you choose not to say that contributed to the situation?" This is a hugely powerful month. Remember, people who fail to plan, plan to fail.

GEMSTONE WISDOM: CITRINE

Citrine, one of the abundance gemstones, is a great teacher for attracting wealth and prosperity. By increasing concentration and kick-starting the mind, this dynamic stone assists in formulating a manifestation strategy. Also known as the "merchant stone" or "success stone", Citrine encourages exploring new possibilities and the joy they can bring. Money and joy – you can't beat that combination!

✷ www.shopBigSky.com ✷

ESSENTIAL OIL APPLICATION:

Connecting with the collective energies this month, we look to the oils that support revelation, adjustment, and manifestation. Some of those beliefs can be tied to money such as "You have to work hard for money.", "I don't deserve this.", or "I can't make enough money doing what I love." Allow the oils selected for you to shift those limiting belief patterns and create a new belief system that serves you. If you have unresolved situations or experiences, the recommended oils for April have the potential to unveil what is hidden and allow it to be healed or processed.

- **Orange -** Diffuse, Diffuse, Diffuse! Place 3 drops in an essential oil diffuser. This oil is a manifesting powerhouse. Bountiful blessings come in many forms. Orange oil supports bringing in abundance. If you have a situation that you have some concern or rumination about, apply 1 - 2 drops of Orange to the palm of your hands, breathe in, and allow this citrus oil to create the harmony of your wishes being fulfilled. This is a sure way to positively set intention and focus for finances or any other positive outcome.

- **Copaiba -** (topical use dilute with carrier oil) 1-2 drops applied over heart/chest area. 1-2 drops at base of skull by hairline to increase awareness. Place 2 drops in a diffuser. Copaiba is truly a powerhouse oil that supports every system in the body. To encourage self-awareness, use this oil to release the hidden aspects of yourself that may be weighing you down. Truly transformative, this oil can reveal your sense of purpose and transmute negative self-talk or thinking into productive insight.

Chakras supported by these oils: Crown, Heart, Root, Sacral

POSITIVE AFFIRMATION/INTENTION:
I am open to unlimited potential. I trust my inner compass to guide me to the people and places that allow me to fulfill my purpose.

MOVEMENT OF THE MONTH: LEGS UP THE WALL

As this month is a month of revealing and adjusting, we look at being in the quiet contemplative state of Viparita Karani, Legs Up the Wall. This pose has been known to have numerous health benefits, such as increasing circulation, decreasing insomnia, lowering blood pressure, to name a few. It also brings relief from stress and anxiety and is calming to the nervous system, allowing us to think more clearly. It also assists with respiratory health, opening the chest and heart chakra, and increasing our ability to listen with the "heart" instead of the mind.

This variation of Viparita Karani uses a support to maximize the health benefits of Legs Up the Wall pose. In order to do it properly, you will need a round bolster or two folded blankets. Additionally, you have to place your legs vertically on any upright support such as a wall. Find your perfect spot by moving your support. Find a placement that feels comfortable for you. When you have finally found that proper placement for your support, which is a few inches from the wall, you can start by sitting sideways to the right side of your support. Your right side should be placed against the wall and floor.

Energy Almanac **2020 Edition**

Begin by taking a deep breath and exhaling. Move your legs up toward the wall while your head and shoulder rest on the floor. For beginners, this pose is a bit difficult to achieve and there is a tendency that you may slide off from your support, but don't be discouraged because you will soon get used to the position. Try to move your support away from the wall or lower your support until you become more comfortable in your position. Your sitting bones should be in a slightly downward position because of the space between the wall and your support. Your front torso should be arched from your pubis to your shoulders. If your front torso looks flat, you may have slipped from the support. To correct this, you have to bend your knees and put your feet up on the wall. Lift your pelvis a few inches away from the support and place the support higher up beneath your pelvis. After the adjustment, you can use the support as you normally would by lowering your pelvis again. Allow your arms to rest about 6-8 inches from your body, with palms facing upward in a receptive manner. Your heart is open as you listen with intention and connect to your breath. Relax your throat. Close your eyes and breathe. You may want soothing music playing to assist with your relaxation as you can stay in this pose for 10 -15 minutes. When you're through, gently roll down to one side, rest, then come to a seated position. Often times we receive insight in these quiet postures. Journaling can be beneficial in reflecting on them.

NOURISHMENT :

Let's talk protein! When all of the collective energies are at play and revealing #allthethings, we need to adjust and manifest. Powering up is often the only way to power through. In addition, the season of spring calls for cleansing the heavy, starchy foods and toxins that have built up during the winter.

Plant-based protein options include chia pudding*, avocados, nuts, seeds, beans, hummus, quinoa, and brown rice. All of these can be added to salads or incorporated into easy-to-grab snacks.

Animal Protein: Aim to have most of your plate filled with plant-based items and use meat as more of a condiment rather than the main course. Buy as local as possible, and remember, you are what you eat, so make sure you are supporting humanely-raised products without growth hormones and with sustainable farming practices. Yes, it's more expensive, but allow less to be more here. Choose quality over quantity.

THE HEALTHY GODMOTHER HINT: Did you know that chickens have the largest adrenal glands per overall weight than any other animal? You know the expression "like a chicken with her head cut off"? Well you can use the "energetics of food" to your advantage! This year is intense, and you're probably finding yourself nursing a vulnerability hangover more often than you'd like. Use the adrenaline that runs through chickens to support your own adrenaline when it's being bottomed out after emotional interactions or when you've put yourself out there in more vulnerable ways. Use chicken as a "step down plan" rather than a crash landing. Plan chicken soup with bone broth or a batch of Nourish Yourself Chicken Salad* after big events.

FOODS THAT NOURISH:

- Sprouts
- Seeds
- Responsibly farmed protein
- Whole grains
- Throat Coat Tea

CHAKRAS AT PLAY: Root, Sacral, Throat

SEASONAL FOCUS:

- Cleansing
- Nourishing Liver & Gallbladder

SEASONAL FOCUS:

- Protein Bites
- Chia Pudding
- Chicken Salad
- Egg Muffins

JOURNAL THIS:

WHAT CONTRIBUTION CAN I BE AND RECEIVE BY LIVING IN ALIGNMENT WITH MY VALUES?
WHAT ARE MY VALUES AND HOW CAN I CHOOSE THEM MORE OFTEN?

Love this information? *Get your own private reading or consultation by visiting the writers' personal websites which can be found in the back of The Energy Almanac.*

April Notes

✯ www.shopBigSky.com ✯

May

EVOLVING MINDS. REVIEW. REFLECT. RENEW.

MAY 4–10

DO CHECK TO BE SURE YOU ARE SUSTAINABLY PREPARED.

DON'T BE PESSIMISTIC ABOUT EXTERNAL FACTORS.

MAY 11–17

DO EXPECT FORWARD MOTION.

DON'T LET YOUR ENERGY BE SCATTERED.

MAY 18–24

DO MANAGE YOUR CAPACITY TO RESPOND THOUGHTFULLY.

DON'T BE SUPERFICIAL.

MAY 25–31

DO BE UPLIFTING WITH YOUR WORDS.

DON'T FOCUS ON WHAT'S WRONG.

MAY 7

FULL MOON IN SCORPIO

ELEVATE YOUR PERSPECTIVE.

MAY 22

NEW MOON IN GEMINI

ADOPT NEW WAYS OF THINKING.

EVOLVING MINDS. REVIEW. REFLECT. RENEW.

This month there is something powerful moving through the human mind. For the next level of transformation to happen, we have to individually and collectively work with the contents of our minds. It's time to release and let go of our reliance on it as a decision making tool. Your mind can keep you stuck in old patterns. It's time to move past that and rely on something much more —your heart! But before you get there, you must redefine what power you give to your mind.

There is a great opportunity to do that now as the nodal axis shifts from Cancer/Capricorn to Gemini/Sagittarius this month. The nodes spend about 18 months in each sign, making it through all 12 signs approximately every 18 years. This means you haven't had an opportunity like this since 2002! The emphasis of Gemini and its ruling planet Mercury this month will help you on your way. All that is required is an open mind and willingness to evolve your thinking.

DATES TO WATCH:

- **May 4, Mercury conjunct Sun in Taurus.** Practical and down-to-earth thinking drives actions. Enjoy the simple pleasures.

- **May 5, Nodal Shift from Cancer/Capricorn to Gemini/Sagittarius.** The North and South Node represents destiny and karma respectively.

- **May 7, Full Moon in Scorpio.** With the Full Moon so close to the Mercury-Sun conjunction, the theme of simplicity continues but is directed toward your finances, making it a great time to pay down debt.

- **May 10, Saturn retrograde in Aquarius.** Saturn has given us a taste of Aquarian genius, but now retrogrades back to Capricorn, ensuring our new reality has a solid foundation.

- **May 11, Mercury into Gemini.** Increase in mind chatter and communication.

- **May 12, Mars into Pisces.** Possible frustration as the mind is moving quickly, but the pace of action slows down now.

- **May 12, Venus retrograde in Gemini.** Dealing with inner contradictions in love, values, and money.

- **May 14, Jupiter retrograde in Capricorn.** Testing and retesting the new structures in our lives. Will they stand the test of time? Are they sustainable?

✦ www.shopBigSky.com ✦

Energy Almanac 2020 Edition

- **May 20, Sun into Gemini.** Communication, networking, social engagements, and a busy mind are all highlighted.

- **May 22, New Moon in Gemini.** Set intentions around communication skills, social agility, and releasing mental anxiety.

- **May 28, Mercury into Cancer.** Emotions added to our thoughts. Moodiness and feelings color our words.

ASTROLOGY BY THE WEEKS:

WEEK 1: MAY 4–10, 2020
Mercury is the busiest planet this week as it delivers new messages to the Sun, shares with Neptune, and dances with both Pluto and Jupiter. There is so much going on in our minds and in what we are communicating.

Mercury's many connections this week spotlight the changes our minds and consciousness are going through. New ideas and new ways of thinking are possible.

This week everyone is experiencing a shift in the path of destiny and karma as the north and south nodes move from the Cancer/Capricorn axis to the Gemini/Sagittarius axis. Our collective destiny is in changing the way we think (Gemini) while becoming more conscious and broadening our definition of "other" through ideological differences (Sagittarius). For the next 18 months you will be confronted personally by the need to expand your thinking and release limiting beliefs.

Saturn retrograde in Aquarius and back into Capricorn is going back to make sure we have learned the lessons of sustainability, resourcefulness, and good stewardship. During the next weeks, he will come ever closer to making the second of three triple conjunctions with Jupiter and Pluto (the first time was in January 2020). Be willing to check within and see that you are prepared personally, and also be prepared for the likely issues you will see in the outer world during the next few months.

Shadow: Sometimes life throws us curve balls, and you move two steps forward and one step back. The tendency is to be upset by it. It's time to see the glass as half full rather than half empty. We are moving forward even if we feel at times like we are not making much progress.

WEEK 2: MAY 11–17, 2020
This is going to be one busy week astrologically! Mercury changes signs, Mars changes signs, Venus turns retrograde, Jupiter turns retrograde and this is all on top of some inner planet transits that are both trying but also empowering.

First up this week is Mercury's (the messenger planet) move into Gemini. You may notice the speed of thought and communication increasing. There is also the possibility of scattering your energy, so take care to focus on what is important.

Next, Mars (planet of action and forward movement) moves into Pisces, where he is not very happy. Mars movement is slowed in Pisces, creating possible frustration at not being able to move forward. The best use of Mars in Pisces is to lean into your creative and imaginative side. Dream and envision what is possible. The time will come in the next 6 weeks for taking dynamic action!

Venus turns retrograde. This is a time to revisit the alignment of your life with your stated values. As Venus is retrograde in Gemini, we're dealing with duality, polarity, and learning to see the two sides of everything. This is also Venus' first retrograde with Uranus in Taurus (Venus rules Taurus), so there are financial considerations we will grapple with, and perhaps a recession or slowing economy. This might be a great time to look at your own personal financial health.

Jupiter is the planet of growth and expansion. When it is in forward motion, we see growth happening for us in the outer world. When it is retrograde, growth turns inward. We might be integrating everything we have seen, heard, practiced, and evolved through during this time. Inner work is favored now.

Perhaps the biggest question of the week as it pertains to the aspects made by the planets is do you want to stay stuck or are you ready to move forward into the new? It bears looking at what you can release from the past versus what you want to take with you as you move on in the spiral of consciousness.

Shadow: Insecurity and fear are shadows that prevent forward motion. You are at a crossroads now and have to choose whether to resist moving forward or embrace change and all its potential.

Week 3: May 18–24, 2020

With the exception of a couple of days this week, it is a much easier week than the last one. The Sun moves into Gemini, and there is a New Moon in Gemini, which adds a fun and sociable energy of the United States Memorial weekend.

The week starts with the Moon in Aries. You may feel primed to get things done, whereas Tuesday may be emotionally volatile as the Moon challenges Pluto, Jupiter, and Saturn. There has been plenty of this energy lately. You should be nearly a pro at managing the emotional waters. This is all about your ability to respond versus reacting to what is going on around you.

Wednesday, the Sun moves into Gemini, and your focus shifts to the more youthful, curious, and social aspects of life. This is a time to follow your ideas and creative impulses, learn new things, and explore the diversity of the people around you. Engage in networking and building new relationships based on mutual interests.

Friday's New Moon, see May Moons below, is busy! Mercury conjuncts Venus, Sun trines Saturn, Mercury squares Neptune, and the Moon has only one challenging aspect, which is a square to Mars. Likely you are feeling hopeful and optimistic. The Moon's square (challenge) to Mars may be an emotional one. Perhaps inner conflict between what you want and what you "see" in life triggers momentary anger or upset. This is an initiating New Moon, and it is up to you to know what you want to create, so be cautious.

Shadow: Superficiality. This whole year is about the deep, lasting changes that must be made in order for us to survive and thrive in the next decades. Don't make change only at the surface of things. Be willing to do the deeper work. Remember the recession of 2008? A bandage was put over the problems and did nothing to change the underlying causes. Demand better of yourself and all leaders to avoid repeating the same mistakes.

Week 4: May 25–31, 2020
The final week of May is smooth sailing with the only major change being Mercury's move into the sign of Cancer.

The Moon moves through Cancer, Leo, and Virgo this week, making her usual rounds of connections. There isn't anything earth shattering, but maybe a few surprises or emotional moments.

Thursday, Mercury moves into Cancer which shifts your mind and your mouth to more emotional and nurturing territory. Mercury in Cancer has a huge capacity to uplift with words. Words have power, and the power now is in the tone and feeling of what you are saying.

Shadow: Are you focusing on the positive or on the negative? This shadow is about making sure we're aware that what we focus on is what we are creating. Be response-able for your own creations. Heal the imbalances in your own life.

. . . .

May Moons

FULL MOON @ 17° SCORPIO/TAURUS | MAY 7, AT 6:46 AM ET

MOON MUSINGS:
The Full Moon is a time for completion, revelation, and releasing. With the Moon in Scorpio you might have been holding on to old emotional wounds, grievances, and fears, and this is a super time to let go. Move forward in your life with a lighter heart and renewed passion.

The degree of the zodiac the Moon sits at suggests that when you change your orientation toward those things you are blessed by and grateful for, something magical happens. You are transformed and then can focus on what is positive in your life. While there is still craziness and a lot of change swirling around, you can rise up, like the owl from this book cover, and see from a higher vantage point. Let go of small thinking and elevate your perspective.

✸ www.shopBigSky.com ✸

NEW MOON @ 2° GEMINI | MAY 22, AT 1:39 PM ET

MOON MUSINGS:

The New Moon is a time of sowing seeds and setting conscious intentions for what comes next. With the Sun-Moon combination in early Gemini, there is the opportunity to form new ways of thinking and a new relationship to the mind. Gemini is also the sign of communication, so the New Moon here also can change the discourse on the planet. What important topics can you be discussing and focusing conversations around?

Gemini's motto is, "I think, therefore I am." Impactful, right? It is a reminder that what you think has a lot of power to shape who you are. Also in Gemini during this New Moon is Venus in retrograde, and Mercury and the North Node assisting in some major rewiring of our minds!

Suggestion for this New Moon: Take a look around you at your outer world. Do you love what you see? Are your relationships awesome? Do you love the work you do? Are you creating abundance in all ways? If not, take some time to look at the contents of your mind and adopt some new ways of thinking.

Resources

NUMEROLOGY: 9 UNIVERSAL MONTH IN A 4 UNIVERSAL YEAR

KEY WORDS: REVIEW, REFLECT, RENEW

Most of us travel with a trunk full of junk. We can't see it, but it's there. Whenever we enter into a 9 cycle like this universal month of 9, we are being asked to open up the trunk and take a look inside. What are you holding on to that needs to get kicked to the curb? Who are you hanging out with who is not in alignment with your plan to move forward? What have you left unfinished that needs to be addressed? What is standing in your way? Is it relationships? Is it stuff? Maybe you have some limiting beliefs about yourself that you need to release. The universal year of 4 is supporting you while you execute a plan for excavating the junk. The 9 universal month is asking you to really look at all the obstacles and limitations that are around you.

GEMSTONE WISDOM: APATITE

Hmm, let me ponder that thought. The clear-minded energy of Apatite encourages reflection and releases confusion. Muddled thoughts be gone. Be flexible and open to the clarity you receive. Apatite is a wonderful stone of self-expression and an excellent way to tap into your hearts desires. Set a new goal and go for it.

ESSENTIAL OIL APPLICATION:

The theme of renew and reflect joins us this month. There are times when we need to revisit the past for a short time, if only to remind us of where we have been. Like looking in the rear-view mirror, it's only intended as a quick reference as the larger vision is moving forward ahead of you. Have you ever noticed thought or feeling patterns that come out of nowhere but you feel they are tied to the past? These could be generational patterns of thought instilled in you from parents or grandparents. Sometimes it can be collective experiences or influences that have shaped us. Allow the oils selected for you to shift those limiting belief patterns and create a new belief system that serves you.

- **Basil -** Apply 2 drops to lower back and 2 drops to the bottom of each foot, paying special attention to the area directly below the ball of your foot. Basil is a welcomed oil when you want to feel rejuvenated and renewed. Sustenance is what one can expect from the natural energy levels this oil can offer. When depletion feels like your theme, or you are proactively working on supporting your energy levels, Basil will definitely be your friend for the long haul.

- **Douglas Fir -** Apply 1-2 drops to pulse points on wrists and breathe in. Douglas Fir can amplify your ability to connect to the truth about your belief then gently and lovingly gives them permission to be released. Be the trailblazer to your dreams and desires. By using this oil, you can let go of what thoughts may be holding you back. Known for its abundant growth patterns, you may notice while using Douglas Fir that your own personal growth is up-leveled.

Chakras supported by these oils: Root, Sacral

POSITIVE AFFIRMATION/INTENTION:

I pull from an unlimited resource of vitality and energy that continues to support me. I imprint my own values and beliefs and release the need to hold onto ideals that others have created for me.

MOVEMENT OF THE MONTH: RECLINING BUTTERFLY

Reclining Butterfly pose, Baddha Konasana, is a quiet, contemplative heart opener. With the energies of renewal and reflection, we intentionally rest in this pose for balance to be the observer. It allows us to stay non-reactive and create an open mind to the many possibilities before us.

You will need a bolster and two folded blankets for this pose. Sitting on the floor, bring the soles of your feet together while bending the knees outward. The sits bones are rooted in the earth and your thighs are open outward as you bring the soles of the feet as close to your pelvis as possible. The bolster is along the spine with it being down as near the sacrum as possible. The folded blankets stay alongside you, in line with your arms, to support them as you recline back onto the bolster. (You may also need to roll a blanket or towel behind your head for support.) As you melt into the pose, your heart opens, and you bring space into the heart chakra. With each breath, connect your intuition with your heart. Be the observer as your thoughts pass by like clouds, allowing them to be released and creating a peaceful balance within.

NOURISHMENT:

This feels like a reset month. Sustainability is popping up over and over. How are you doing with your 80/20 rule? Another way to support the long haul of this whole "nourish yourself for life" thing is meal planning and prepping. Cook once and eat twice or even thrice! It's a game changer in most houses. Cook up extra roasted veggies and make lots of sides 2-3 nights in a row and then mix and match the rest of the week. Add some quinoa or brown rice to what once went with sweet potato. Add a salad and poof! Another night of dinner success. There's no better feeling than knowing the answer to the dreaded question, "What's for dinner?", except when you realize most of it is already made!

The other place to focus on this time of year is cleansing. This can be a loaded word and means different things to different people. From a Chinese Five Element Theory perspective, the organs to focus on in the spring are the liver and gallbladder. These organs represent anger, stress, and grief. Got any of that? (I thought so.) Cleansing these organs is key, and the easiest way is with warm water and lemon (use organic and leave the rind right in the water for optimal benefits). Green tea is also great for this, so if you've incorporated the Morning Elixir* mentioned back in January, then you're ahead of the game and can add additional cleansing support with dandelion root tea and/or milk thistle.

THE HEALTHY GODMOTHER HINT: Do you dry brush? It's yet another way to cleanse your system without taking radical measures with elimination diets or fasting. Use a skin brush to loosen toxins in and under the skin, flush the lymphatic system, and reduce the appearance of cellulite. Begin at fingertips and toes and move in circular motions toward your heart.

FOODS THAT NOURISH:

- Smoothies
- Sprouts
- Dandelion greens (sautéed in coconut oil with a drizzle of raw honey)

SEASONAL FOCUS:

- Nourishing Liver & Gallbladder
- Adding in more raw food

CHAKRAS AT PLAY: Sacral, Heart, Throat

RECIPES:

- Morning Elixir
- Pineapple Mango Salsa
- Fiddlehead Salad

JOURNAL THIS:

WHERE IN MY LIFE HAVE I BEEN PREDICTING FUTURES IN PLACE OF ALLOWING INFINITE POSSIBILITIES?

Love this information? Get your own private reading or consultation by visiting the writers' personal websites which can be found in the back of The Energy Almanac.

May Notes

Energy Almanac 2020 Edition

June

RIGOR. ACTION. CONCENTRATION. PLANNING.

JUNE 1-7

DO COMMUNICATE YOUR DESIRES WITHIN RELATIONSHIPS.
DON'T PUSH BEYOND YOUR OWN LIMITS.

JUNE 8-14

DO EXPECT EMOTIONAL VOLATILITY.
DON'T START ANYTHING NEW AND DON'T PUSH.

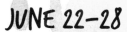

REST YOUR BEST

JUNE 15-21

DO BE PATIENT.
DON'T FORGET TO CELEBRATE SUMMER SOLSTICE.

JUNE 22-28

DO PAY ATTENTION TO INTUITION AND CREATE A PLAN.
DON'T PASS JUDGEMENT.

MERCURY RETROGRADES

SLOW DOWN!

My Plan

JUNE 5

FULL MOON LUNAR ECLIPSE IN SAGITTARIUS
MOVE IN A DIRECTION GUIDED BY SOURCE.

JUNE 21

NEW MOON-SOLAR ECLIPSE IN CANCER
ALIGNMENT WITH WHAT'S NEW.

 www.shopBigSky.com

June

RIGOR. ACTION. CONCENTRATION. PLANNING.

One word comes to mind to describe the month of June - rigorous. So much happens this month. Some things are subtle and operating in the background, while others are right in your face and creating tension and stress. Overall, the best way to deal with the ups and downs of the month is to keep tuned in to your own inner voice. Release any resistance to change, be kind and generous with your time and attention, and practice self-love and self-care throughout the month. Next month we will have some integration time before the August-December window ramps things up again.

DATES TO WATCH:

- **June 5, Full Moon-Lunar Eclipse.** With the nodal axis shift last month, the eclipse pattern now moves across Gemini-Sagittarius. See June Moons below.

- **June 11, Sun challenges Neptune.** Rest your best.

- **June 18, Mercury Retrograde.** Mercury is retrograde from June 18-July 27 in Cancer. Nurture and take care of yourself and family. Do things that support your traditions.

- **June 20, Summer/Winter Solstice and Sun's move into Cancer.** Nurturing, home, family and traditions take center stage.

- **June 21, New Moon-Solar Eclipse.** The New Moon gives opportunities to set intentions on what you want to manifest. A solar eclipse adds power and punch to our intention setting. See June Moons below.

- **June 22, Neptune turns retrograde.** We now have easy access to our intuition and instincts. Pay close attention to what is coming up in your dreams.

- **June 25, Venus turns direct.** Hopefully you've spent time honing your values and working through relationship and financial issues. This suggests you now get to demonstrate the lessons you've learned out into the world.

- **June 27, Mars moves into Aries.** The planet of action is at home in the sign of Aries. Expect activity and movement to increase.

✸ www.shopBigSky.com ✸

ASTROLOGY BY THE WEEKS:

WEEK 1: JUNE 1–7, 2020
The first week of June is a busy one with the inner planets making many connections to one another, the Full Moon, and the first lunar eclipse across Gemini-Sagittarius.

There is a busy week ahead in relationships and in communication. Venus is retrograde in Gemini squaring Mars in Pisces. Communicating your needs and desires as they relate to your physical relationships with one another is primary now. Don't be afraid to get creative and imaginative in the bedroom.

Venus also dances with the Sun this week and that means love and affection received and given. If you are unattached, don't be surprised if a previous love relationship is rekindled or if someone from your past reaches out to connect.

Next up is the Full Moon-Lunar Eclipse, the first across the sign of Gemini-Sagittarius in this series. This eclipse sets the tone for what our lessons over the next 18 months will be about.

Take care this weekend as your physical energies are running high, which could push you into doing things that are beyond your endurance or physical capability.

Shadow: Narrow-mindedness and self-righteousness. Both of these energies come from the new focus on the Gemini-Sagittarius axis. In its shadow, Gemini can get caught up in its own stuck way of thinking. Sagittarius self-righteously refuses to see other points of view as valid. Release the limits and embrace it all.

WEEK 2: JUNE 8–14, 2020
This week the Moon moves through Capricorn, Aquarius, Pisces, and Aries. There are only two major connections between planets. The Sun challenges Neptune and Mars conjuncts Neptune.

There is some emotional volatility to begin the week as the Moon in Capricorn joins up with Pluto, Jupiter, and Saturn, the trio of planets that have been shaking up our world this year. You may be feeling fatigued by the drama in the outer world.

The Sun challenges Neptune to a game of "Rest Your Best" as we may be feeling low energy and tired. Take the day off if possible (June 11) or find ways to recharge your batteries. Sun-Neptune and Mars-Neptune (on Saturday) can also make you feel discouraged at the state of the world. Take heart. This feeling will pass fairly quickly. Try to avoid starting anything new until next week.

Shadow: Inappropriate use of force. When we are feeling down or discouraged, we can try to counter that energy by using force or willpower. This just leads to burnout and frustration. Instead, this week is best used in peaceful, quiet pursuits. If something is not happening naturally and easily, let go of force and put your energy, time, and attention on something else. Try meditation, yoga, or other physical/spiritual activities that recharge your body, mind, and spirit.

Energy Almanac **2020 Edition**

✬ www.shopBigSky.com ✬

Week 3: June 15–21, 2020

The Moon begins in action-oriented Aries, and you'll want to get things done. Then Mars connects with Pluto on the same day Mercury turns retrograde. The week ends at the Summer/Winter Solstice and the New Moon Solar Eclipse at the critical degree of zero Cancer.

You know that feeling of going nowhere when you have your feet both on the gas pedal and the brake? You may feel like that this week. You'll want to get things done, and the energy is there, but Mercury turning retrograde spoils the party by slowing things down. Grrrr! The reason for the slowdown may be found in the closing of both a lunar cycle and a seasonal cycle. Be patient until later in the week when the New Moon opens up pathways of action for everyone.

New Moon comes on the heels of the Summer/Winter Solstice. Expect that there is going to be a lot of energy exchanged the last few days of this week. The Solstice point holds the promise of the new and then so does the Moon. Mars is currently involved with almost every planet. That means you can expect a lot of action and conflict as Mars stimulates the ego in everyone. If you're in the USA, this is likely going to show up in rhetoric and/or debates in the run for President.

Shadow: Turbulence and crisis is the shadow of the week. You can either get dragged into the traumas and dramas of the world or choose peace. As more people choose peace, the greater the likelihood that we can experience it rather than the conflict implied by this week's shadow. Do take a part in creating a better world.

Week 4: June 22–28, 2020

There are still some important changes taking place. Neptune, planet of spirituality, turns retrograde, Venus ends her retrograde by turning direct, and later in the week, Mars moves into Aries, his home sign, before meeting up with Saturn.

Neptune in retrograde supports hearing your inner voice. Listen to your intuition now as it may be relaying vital information to you. If you don't listen now, in the fall when Neptune turns back to direct motion, you may wish you had as the reason for the intuition becomes clear.

Venus ends her retrograde, but you may still be integrating new values and feeling the effects of any financial setbacks experienced in the retrograde. Financial news is likely prominent now.

Mars moving into his own sign is preparing for his retrograde cycle. Even though he doesn't retrograde until September, pay attention now to what is opening up for you. Know that anything new you begin now will encounter a slow down or re-evaluation period this fall when Mars retrogrades. It is still okay to take action and move forward!

The day after Mars moves into Aries, he forms a supportive aspect with Saturn. If you are to take forward steps, you must have a strategy for getting where you want to go. Take the time to create that plan now. You'll be glad you did.

Shadow: Watch for polarized judgment of anything and anyone. Ego energies are running high this week, so be very cautious in how you work with others. Be aware that others may also be working from their egos. Have compassion for people who haven't yet learned this lesson.

. . . .

June Moons

FULL MOON –LUNAR ECLIPSE @ 15° SAGITTARIUS | JUNE 5, AT 6:13 PM ET

MOON MUSINGS:

The Full Moon gives you the opportunity to let go of what isn't serving you, complete unfinished business, and become enlightened by what is truly important to you. This Full Moon is also an eclipse, allowing even more opportunity to let go of the old and move forward. Letting go allows you to be lighter and more aligned with your higher self.

The Moon during this eclipse is very near the south node (past, karma) and that means what you let go of around grievances, patterns, subconscious motivations, or whatever baggage you are carrying, is from the past.

Both the Sun and the Moon during the eclipse are squaring (challenging) Mars and Neptune in Pisces. You are being challenged to live by higher ideals and move in a direction guided by a higher power. These 4 planets form an aspect pattern called a T-square. In this case, it is Mars/Neptune in Pisces that form the point, meaning we need to move to Virgo in order to find the solutions to our challenge. Virgo means practical, organized, purified, and healthy ways of being. It also means taking action and not just dreaming of what could be. Releasing is only one part of the equation this Full Moon. You actually have to take steps too.

The Full Moon/Lunar Eclipse in Sagittarius/Gemini is also a prelude to the next Jupiter-Pluto conjunction (coming up June 30th) that is transforming society and societal structures. There is a lot of old cultural, ideological, and institutional transformations happening simultaneously. Big changes and powerful planetary transits can create stress, so remember to engage self-love, self-care, compassion, and meditation to help you along the way. See this month's nourishment article.

NEW MOON–SOLAR ECLIPSE @ 0° CANCER | JUNE 21, AT 2:42 AM ET

MOON MUSINGS:

Are you ready for another eclipse? June has been a fairly rigorous month in terms of the astrological signatures, but here we have a New Moon-Solar Eclipse in Cancer, both opening up opportunities for the new while simultaneously linking us to our past errant actions and behaviors.

While a New Moon opens a portal for new beginnings, this one is also a solar eclipse which adds power and punch. This is also the last eclipse in the Cancer/Capricorn series that so upset the balance of power and authority in our governments and institutions. You are either aligned with the new or are stubbornly holding on to the past. One leads to peace, the other to continued unrest and polarization.

Believe it or not, the same T-square that was operating during the Full Moon is also quite active now. But instead of the Sun and Moon holding the tension of opposites, it is the north and the south nodes (destiny and karma). It seems to ask, "What do you want to create?" The tone and tenor of the next 18 months is being set with this New Moon. All is possible, and it is up to you to choose. Choose well. You will live with the results of those choices, for better or worse, for the foreseeable future.

. . . .

Resources

NUMEROLOGY: 1 UNIVERSAL MONTH IN A 4 UNIVERSAL YEAR

KEY WORDS: ACTION, CONCENTRATION, PLANNING

It's GO TIME this month! This is probably your best, most promising month of 2020. The 1 universal month says, "Let's get dirty and plant some seeds so we can get a plan in motion." The 4 universal year says, "Heck yeah, I'm game! I'll even help you with your plot plan!" These two energies are in great harmony with one another. The 1 says start it and the 4 says it will be well supported. Remember that anything you give your energy, attention, and focus to gets bigger. This is a month where you can really concentrate on what you want to start. What a great lineup. This is the month to put a solid foundation underneath anything you are planning to manifest.

GEMSTONE WISDOM: LAPIS LAZULI

The energy of Lapis Lazuli is all about taking charge, saying what you need to say (without reservation), and letting the world know who you really are. This month you'll need to roll with it and remain self-aware through all the changes. Follow your inner voice on how best to navigate the changes and be true to yourself. Lapis Lazuli provides clarity and insight which are wonderful tools to create a plan of action. Go forth and conquer!

ESSENTIAL OIL APPLICATION:

Are you ready? This is the time for action, concentration, and planning. Pulling from your experiences last month when you were reflecting, the oils selected for June can thrust you into action while planning your steps. The fast-pace call to action that you may feel right now also requires focus. Luckily, we've got you covered with nature's best cheerleader essential oils.

✯ www.shopBigSky.com ✯

- **Blue Tansy -** (topical use dilute with carrier oil) 1 drop to bottom of each big toe. May also apply 1-2 drops behind ears, back of neck, or over solar plexus. In a month poised for action, or when inspired action is needed, Blue Tansy helps to break through any hesitation or procrastination. When you are unsure of the next step to take, or if you are overwhelmed with the pending to do list, Blue Tansy can be the catalyst to take the next step forward.

- **Focus Blend -** A blend of Amyris, Patchouli, Frankincense, Lime, Ylang Ylang, Sandalwood, and Roman Chamomile. Apply 1 -2 drops to back of neck toward top of spine. May also apply 2 drops to the bottom of each foot or big toes. This powerful blend of oils is quite the multi-tasker. Focus Blend supports both feeling grounded and staying connected in thought. It will bring awareness and attention to the task at hand, allowing side thoughts or distractions to fall away.

Chakras supported by these oils: Crown, Brow, Throat, Solar Plexus, Sacral, Root

POSITIVE AFFIRMATION/INTENTION:
My awareness is in the here and now. I am focused and see the desired outcome already complete. Thank you.

MOVEMENT OF THE MONTH: CORPSE POSE

June is the month for quiet reflection while being present. Savasana, or Corpse pose, is the pose for the month. Ahhh yes, our sweet surrender.

The energies for June bring the need for this relaxation pose. Lying on your back with a bolster under your knees (if you have any low back concerns), rest your arms at your sides a bit away from your body. The neck is supported under your cervical spine with a small rolled towel. Feet are resting a bit more than hip width apart. If you'd prefer, cover yourself with a blanket and/or an eye pillow to help contain your energy. Connect with your breath, feeling your belly rise and fall. Stay with the breath, being in the room, relaxed yet not asleep. Surrender as you breathe in clarity and peace. You may want to play soft music or a guided meditation as you begin to cultivate your daily practice of Savasana.

NOURISHMENT :

There is a call for a lot of self-care and self-love this moon cycle, and there is a third "self" that often gets forgotten: self-trust. Who knows which comes first... it's kind of like the organic chicken and egg. Either way it's an intricate player within the trifecta. They don't exist independently of each other and trust can be a hard thing to get your head around. Give Brene Brown's talk "The Anatomy of Trust" a listen. She talks about all the ways you can build trust with those around you and it got me thinking... Maybe we can only really trust others once we have learned to really trust ourselves. Boom. Mic drop. Next thought: What does that even look and feel like? If you don't know, then maybe you need a Self-Trust Jar*.

✴ www.shopBigSky.com ✴

Brene says, trust is built in the tiny "marble jar moments" and the same is true when building it with yourself. It's built in all the micro moments and ways you show up for yourself, helping you shine more brightly. It's seeking internal validation vs. external validation and setting healthy boundaries as well as being mindful of your energetic inputs and outputs. It's choosing a cup of lavender and chamomile tea instead of a bowl of ice cream before bed... and it's trusting yourself to have that bowl of ice cream when you really want it. It's staying with yourself when things feel hard and scary and all you want to do is abandon ship. It's that feeling of showing up as you are and feeling so aligned and in your body that it looks feels like you're floating on a cloud. Pretty cool right? Create a Summer Solstice/New Moon ritual with this fun Self-Trust Jar* craft/recipe. Invite your friends. Sit on the deck, drink kombucha and discuss on this longest day!

THE HEALTHY GODMOTHER HINT: Looking for ways to embody all the yin of the Full Moon? Place a jar of filtered water out in the light of the Full Moon, and allow it to infuse all the goodness and then use it as a base for your morning smoothie* or keep it refrigerated for nourishment later in the month.

FOODS THAT NOURISH:

- Berries
- Nuts & Seeds

SEASONAL FOCUS:

- Transition from Spring to Summer

CHAKRAS AT PLAY: Sacral and Solar Plexus

RECIPES:

- Green Juice
- Moon Juice Smoothie
- Nourish Yourself Breakfast Bowl
- Self-Trust Jar

JOURNAL THIS:

WHAT ENERGY CAN I BE THAT WILL CREATE AND GENERATE A PLAN THAT WILL MANIFEST WITH EASE?

Love this information? Get your own private reading or consultation by visiting the writers' personal websites which can be found in the back of The Energy Almanac.

June Notes

Energy Almanac 2020 Edition

July

RESTORING ORDER. CHILL. REST. NURTURE.

JUNE 29–JULY 5

Do become mindful of co-creation.

Don't be rigid or critical.

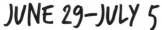

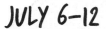

WATCH FOR EMOTIONAL TRIGGERS

JULY 6–12

Do discover why you're being triggered.

Don't fight.

JULY 13–19

Do commit to going with the flow.

Don't be hesitant to move forward with change.

Recharge

JULY 20–26

Do rewrite your old sob stories

Don't stay stuck in old thinking.

OLD ? new

JULY 27–AUGUST 2

Do release emotional tension through laughter or tears.

Don't get sucked into others drama.

TAKE A HIGHER PERSPECTIVE

Drama

JULY 5

FULL MOON LUNAR ECLIPSE IN CANCER

Potential for confusion.

JULY 20

NEW MOON IN CANCER

A choice point.

Energy Almanac 2020 Edition

July

RESTORING ORDER. CHILL. REST. NURTURE.

July presents us with chaotic energy initially, then eases back to give us a chance to breathe a little, then builds again toward the end of the month. We begin the month with Saturn (planet of duty and responsibility) in retrograde, making it back into the sign of Capricorn, where he will again conjunct Jupiter and Pluto. This is all part of a very long-term cycle that we haven't witnessed in several thousand years, so it is important!

Mid-month, Mercury turns direct, releasing us from miscommunication and mind issues. You can finally feel like moving forward again. Mercury Direct is followed by the New Moon in Cancer, and then the Sun moves into Leo. All in all, these are the transits that lighten us up and relieve us from some of the crazy energy we have been witnessing. The last week of the month is somewhat edgy and leads us into a challenging August.

DATES TO WATCH:

- **July 1, Saturn retrograde back into Capricorn.** Relearning or solidifying new lessons as Saturn finishes his trek through Capricorn. Saturn then moves toward another of his epic triple conjunctions with Jupiter and Pluto next month.

- **July 4-5, Full Moon-Lunar Eclipse.** A minor eclipse but is affecting us in the USA. What can you let go of?

- **July 12, Mercury turns direct.** The natural flow and order of the Universe is restored as the messenger planet moves forward once more.

- **July 20, New Moon in Cancer.** In a world that is in flux, what is most important to you? Set intentions in those areas of your life.

- **July 22, Sun moves into Leo.** Time for fun, play, being your individual self, love and romance.

ASTROLOGY BY THE WEEKS:

WEEK 1: JUNE 29 – JULY 5, 2020

This week there is a powerful Jupiter conjunct Pluto in Capricorn, Mercury conjunct Sun, and a Mercury-Sun sextile Uranus. The week is rounded out with another Full Moon-Lunar Eclipse in Capricorn.

The Moon begins the week in Scorpio, deepening and intensifying everything you feel about what is going on. A storm of epic proportions is upon us, catalyzing change and propelling us forward to a new way of being with one another on this planet. Go kicking and screaming or agree to co-create something of lasting value. The Jupiter-Pluto conjunction sets the tone for what comes next.

Later in the week, there is a Full Moon Lunar Eclipse in Cancer. More change, more letting go, more evolution. See July Moons below. You are fast learning the power of co-creation.

Shadow: Avoid being rigid or critical. Begin the process of working together and letting go of old systems that are skewed to benefit only a few rather than everyone equally.

WEEK 2: JULY 6–12, 2020

This week has fewer astrological transits to contend with. Mercury, still in retrograde, challenges Mars and then turns to forward motion.

If you're still reeling from some of last week's transits, this week will come as a welcome change as everything calms down. The Moon makes several difficult connections this week, making it a sure bet that your emotions could be triggered. Attempt to keep balance and equanimity. Don't let your emotions overwhelm you, but definitely dig into what is triggering you.

Mercury challenging Mars is a part of the potential emotional landscape, as he (Mercury) is transiting through Cancer (emotions). Also, Mars in Aries could be the trigger to your emotions. Deal with what is coming up in you without being reactive.

By the end of the week, Mercury is moving forward again, and the Sun is in a calming relationship to Neptune. Escape into a good book, a peaceful environment like the beach or forest, or go see a good movie. Recharge yourself and gain perspective.

Shadow: Fighting, conflict, and greed. Fight, as a shadow, happens to be the struggle to move forward. When you choose your battles wisely, progress is made, but if everything becomes a battle or fight, you soon tire and get angry and disheartened. The shadow of greed is a little more difficult to pin down and deal with as it is a more collective shadow than a personal shadow, yet, it is driving the changes we are struggling through right now. Greed is born from lack and scarcity thinking. Remember the universal Law of Abundance. There is always enough for everyone.

Week 3: July 13–19, 2020

The Sun in Cancer this week opposes the Jupiter-Pluto conjunction, energizing the social changes brought about by the conjunction. How you respond depends on your personal perspective.

Any planet or point moving through Aries, Cancer, or Libra right now challenges the powerful Jupiter-Pluto-Saturn stellium in Capricorn. We begin the week with the Moon in Aries challenging both Saturn and Pluto. There are powerful emotions rippling through the collective.

Later in the week, the Sun in Cancer opposes the planets in Capricorn. Oppositions literally pull you in two different directions. In this case, you can go with the flow of change occurring or stay stuck in fear and become overly protective of what is no longer working. Change is inevitable and no amount of protectionism or wishing for the "good ol' days" is going to help the situation. Get on the bus or step aside.

As the week comes to a close, you are definitely feeling better. Maybe it's curiosity or perhaps hope that changes the atmosphere. Or are you finally willing to transcend differences and come together for the good of the collective?

Shadow: The dominant shadow this week is … wait for it …. psychosis! If you are hesitant to move forward, then you are doomed to repeat the same mistakes again. One popular definition of psychosis or insanity, is doing the same things and expecting a different result. It's time for radical change. Don't hesitate or you'll be stuck in the level of consciousness that created the problem.

Week 4: July 20–26, 2020

This week the Sun opposes Saturn, there is a New Moon in Cancer, the Sun moves into Leo, and Mercury shares energy with Uranus.

This week has the potential to be a good one if you are willing to use the Sun opposing Saturn energy to roll up your sleeves and get some work done. Part of that work is in the New Moon where you can set some powerful intentions to manifest positive outcomes.

Wednesday there is an energy shift with the Sun moving into more jovial, playful Leo. Take a vacation or at least take some time off in the next 30 days while the Sun is in territory that can be rejuvenating.

By Friday, the Moon is in Libra, and that stimulates challenging emotional connections to the trio of planets in Capricorn. Again, keep perspective, be responsible for your own emotional health, and try to create win-win situations with the people in your life.

Shadow: What's your story? The Sun during this time period reminds us of our shared ancestry and evolutionary story. But everyone has their own story to tell. You might speak about your difficult childhood, or issues with relationships, money or work. The more you focus on the "story", the more you hold it in place and it becomes your continuous reality. Begin now to create the new story you want to emerge from your experience of the past.

WEEK 5: JULY 27–AUGUST 2, 2020

The week begins on a busy note. Jupiter, Neptune, Venus, Mercury, and Mars all make connections on Monday, followed by two days of calm, then an edgy Thursday through Sunday.

Monday's energy is all over the place, making for a busy start to this week. Jupiter and Neptune have a philosophical chat, while Venus is challenged to bring unconditional love into relationships, while Mercury and Mars have words! It's likely there may be a clash of ideologies that sparks terse conversations, or you may be really learning to value one another's ideas and differences.

Tuesday and Wednesday are the best days of the week, but there may be some emotional release now as well. Have a good cry or a good laugh. Both work for releasing tension.

Thursday and Friday (July 30-31) are the dates set for the Democratic Party's presidential debates. Mercury opposes Jupiter and trines Neptune those days. You are likely to hear a lot about the Spirit of America and the philosophy that we must adopt to protect the ideals of this nation. Expect a lot of "debate" at this debate, but don't be pulled into drama with the people around you. There is enough room to value each other's ideas, thoughts, and opinions.

The Moon is in Capricorn over the weekend, which means something deeply emotional is moving through you. It might be a good weekend to have projects to work on. You can be task oriented and get a lot done, allowing you to process your emotions without having to hurt other people's feelings.

Shadow: Rise above trauma and drama. What would happen if you used the potential challenges you are experiencing right now as catalysts to making a better world? When you're dragged into the drama of events, you lose the ability to be open-minded.

．．．

July Moons

FULL MOON–LUNAR ECLIPSE @ 13° CANCER | JULY 5, AT 12:45 AM EDT (9:45 PM PT ON JULY 4)

MOON MUSINGS:

Although in this lunar eclipse the earth's shadow doesn't completely cover the Moon, there is still the potential for release, completion, and/or revelation in this Full Moon. Everything about this Moon is "off" and that means potential for confusion, crisis, and conflict. Aspects being made between the planets are not quite exact, but they are close enough to be triggers.

Energy Almanac 2020 Edition

Solution? Lean into your spiritual practice. Use whatever it is that calms and centers you so that you can have clarity about what is correct for you to let go of. Try not to get sucked into the collective angst of outer world events.

NEW MOON @ 28° CANCER | JULY 20, AT 1:34 PM EDT

MOON MUSINGS:

We have reached a tipping point, a crossroads, or in the words of Gregg Braden, American new age author, "a choice point." We have been building toward a change in our systems, structures, governments, laws, and institutions. It's time to decide what direction we go. Do we align with our values? Do we round the corner to the next level of our evolution? Or do we stay stuck in the old divisive and polarizing past? To be clear, rounding the corner does not mean that we are done by any stretch of the imagination. It is going to be up to us as individuals to stay vigilant about the course we take next.

Individually, this Moon presents you with many opportunities to do new things and to affect change. You have choices and power; all you need to do is apply your will and magic can happen.

....

Resources

NUMEROLOGY: 2 UNIVERSAL MONTH IN A 4 UNIVERSAL YEAR

KEY WORDS: CHILL, RESTORE, NURTURE

You may want to get cozy under that beach umbrella this month. July promises to feel much heavier than June did. June had you wanting to plant some seeds and get things rolling, but forget about trying to continue with that same amount of energy. A 2 universal month is a time to hang out in your time-out chair. You are being asked to chill out after a very busy expenditure of energy last month. You need to rest and restore. If you try to punch your way through this month with the same energy and enthusiasm you had in June, you will be sadly disappointed when you don't have what is necessary to advance into the full speed ahead of August. So, do yourself a favor by getting comfy and simply pondering your progress thus far. Nurture the crops you planted last month.

GEMSTONE WISDOM: ROSE QUARTZ

The loving energy of Rose Quartz is the perfect gemstone to pamper your awesome self. Dubbed the love stone, Rose Quartz's gentleness is a soothing treatment to restore and nurture. Hold this gentle yet powerful gemstone over your heart and feel into its healing energy. Breathe deeply and experience its warmth throughout your body. Enjoy your loving energy hug!

ESSENTIAL OIL APPLICATION:

As we settle in to what July brings for us, we have an opportunity to restore and nurture ourselves. You've been busy planning and preparing, and as the tides ebb and flow, we must take time to replenish our resources and give back to ourselves so that we can be the best version of ourselves for others. When chaos sparks up around you, it may be best to focus inward to give yourself the nurturing you deserve and to allow for more resilience when things feel uncertain. The oils chosen for you this month will be supporting you in the areas of your body/soul that most need attention.

- **Turmeric -** Apply 1 drop with a carrier oil over liver and lower back (sacrum). You may also wish to apply 1-2 drops to the bottom of each foot. Turmeric is one of the most restorative oils on the planet. It has been used for thousands of years and is widely known for its powerful anti-inflammatory benefits. Implementing this oil when cleansing, when regeneration is your goal, can prove to have super- charged results. Mood balancing and clearing what is not wanted or needed can be the payoff of using Tumeric.

- **Myrrh -** Apply 2 drops to the heart area and 1 drop to the inside of the elbows (carrier oil recommended). The nurturing, loving energy of Myrrh reminds us of our maternal connection. A mother nurtures, cares for, and unconditionally loves. With loving guidance, this sacred oil can help you care for and nurture yourself. Myrrh invites you to trust that you are moving forward on the right path, and it can align you to do so. You may use myrrh to feel safe, connected, and supported.

Chakras supported by these oils: Solar Plexus, Crown, Root

POSITIVE AFFIRMATION/INTENTION:

I honor my body and soul. I am listening to what they need, and I am offering nurturing love to both in this moment.

MOVEMENT OF THE MONTH: HEAD TO KNEE POSE

The name Janu Sirsasana comes from the Sanskrit words 'Janu' meaning 'knee', 'Sirsa' meaning 'head' and 'asana' meaning 'posture'. This forward fold allows us to see things as they are in the present moment.

Have a yoga block or chair close by for this pose. Sit on your mat with a folded blanket under you. Slide to the edge of the blanket so the sits bones are grounded for forward folding. Extend your legs in front of you. Bend the right knee and bring the right heel to the inner right thigh and the right toes to the left inner thigh. Your left leg is extended and active as we push through our metatarsals and open the back of our knee toward the earth. Lifting your arms overhead, inhale and lengthen your spine, folding forward from your hips to bring your belly button toward your left leg. Root down with your left femur bone. Take your shoulders down away from your ears. Beginners take the forehead to the block or chair placed in line with your extended leg or for those that are flexible, forehead to knee, leading with your heart. Rest in the pose 3-5 breaths. Exhale and gently come up as you root down with your sits bones. Release and do the other side.

NOURISHMENT:

This month is coming in hot in all the ways possible, so let's talk inflammation!

There are many ways inflammation shows up in your body: joint pain & stiffness, autoimmune illness, skin irritations/acne, allergies, fatigue, anxiety, depression, digestive issues.

The foods that create the most inflammation are sugar, high fructose corn syrup, gluten, dairy, highly processed foods, and corn.

How to cool things off? #chill #restore #nurture and...

Enjoy foods rich in omega 3s:
- Chia, flax
- Avocados
- Salmon
- Local Happy Eggs

THE HEALTHY GODMOTHER HINT: Make watermelon and basil kabobs for a snack or fun party offering. They cool things off, hydrate, and the basil provides a cleansing vibe, decreases inflammation, and is rich in omega 3s.

FOODS THAT NOURISH:
- Fresh local fruits & berries
- Farmers' market finds
- Eat the rainbow
- Salmon & peas

SEASONAL FOCUS:
- Staying cool & hydrated
- Nourishing heart & intestine

CHAKRAS AT PLAY: Solar Plexus, Crown

RECIPES:
- Chia Pudding
- Chocolate Avocado Pudding

JOURNAL THIS:

WHAT WOULD IT BE LIKE TO BE COMPLETELY RELAXED? WHAT CHANGE CAN I BE TO REST WITH EASE?

Love this information? Get your own private reading or consultation by visiting the writers' personal websites which can be found in the back of The Energy Almanac.

 www.shopBigSky.com

July Notes

August

PREPARING. DETAILS. SOCIALIZE. EXPRESSION.

AUGUST 3-9
DO STEP TOWARD WHAT IS NEW OR UNUSUAL.
DON'T SLIP INTO FEAR MODE.

AUGUST 10-16
DO PRACTICE RESPONDING OVER REACTING.
DON'T STAY IN POWER STRUGGLES.

AUGUST 17-23
DO GET PRACTICAL; NEATEN UP YOUR LIFE.
DON'T SKIMP ON SPIRITUAL NOURISHMENT.

AUGUST 24-30
DO SEEK HELP WITH THE FEAR YOU FEEL.
DON'T BE IMPATIENT.

be grounded

AUGUST 3
FULL MOON IN AQUARIUS
EMBRACE WHAT IS INNOVATIVE.

AUGUST 18
NEW MOON IN LEO
DEVELOPING CONFIDENCE.

August

PREPARING. DETAILS. SOCIALIZE. EXPRESSION.

August contains the usual round of ups and downs in the astrological landscape. The big difference is the movement of Mars into the degree span in Aries where he will be challenging the Saturn, Pluto, Jupiter conjunction in Capricorn. While this begins with August it will continue onward through the month of December and into early January 2021. Mars will move through its retrograde cycle beginning in September and is why this four-month period has possible conflict, confrontation, and discord. We are fast approaching the crescendo of the shift energy that began in 2016. The transits have been shared here as positively as possible, but there is much potential for the crazier expression of these transits. For you personally, the best route from August through December is to focus on your values, on being open-minded and inclusive, and on what fulfills you and makes you happy.

DATES TO WATCH:

- **August 3, Full Moon in Aquarius.** Make way for the new and innovative by releasing the old and outdated.

- **August 4, Mercury into Leo.** Theatrical, dramatic, and grandiose speaking characterizes Mercury in Leo.

- **August 7, Venus into Cancer.** Show your love through nurturing and protecting. You may feel more emotionally warm and fuzzy.

- **August 15, Uranus turns retrograde.** Watch for contrary behaviors.

- **August 18, New Moon in Leo.** A time of renewed confidence, generosity, and open-heartedness.

- **August 19, Mercury into Virgo.** You may become more detail oriented and analytical, but don't lose sight of the big picture by getting lost in the details.

- **August 22, Sun into Virgo.** Organize, simplify, clean out the closets, and purify your environment. Don't forget to purify your body!

Energy Almanac 2020 Edition

ASTROLOGY BY THE WEEKS:

WEEK 1: AUGUST 3–9, 2020

We start the week with the Full Moon in Aquarius with Mercury and Saturn in an opposition. Then Mars challenges Jupiter from Aries to Capricorn, where, for the next 4 months, we deal with Mars' triggers to planets in Capricorn. The rest of the week is fairly quiet with only the Moon making its usual connections.

The Full Moon in Aquarius presents us with the opportunity to let go of the old and connect to what is new, unusual, innovative, and inventive. But Mercury in Leo opposing more traditional-bound Saturn is sure to have us holding on to the old.

From August to December this year, Mars (warrior planet) challenges the host of planets in Capricorn. Expect conflict, confrontation, ratcheted-up rhetoric, and potentially, further polarization in general which carries us through the presidential election in the USA. Barring any unforeseen catastrophes which have the effect of drawing us together, we are in for quite the ride the next 4 months. Be prepared with your spiritual practice to get you through the days, weeks, and months ahead.

The first taste of this energy is on August 4 when Mars squares (challenges) Jupiter from Aries to Capricorn. Avoid taking risks or overdoing anything. In the outer world, it's possible that radical forces get expressed. Don't fear! Also note that Mars is slowing down for his upcoming retrograde cycle which means what we are dealing with now is likely going to be with us for several months.

Shadow: Division. Who are you following as leaders? Do they promote or present you with opportunities for unity or bringing people together? This week's shadow has Leo narcissistic overtones based in hierarchical thinking. You have to confront where you personally are feeling divided or polarized and heal that. When enough of us have healed the inner division, pathways will open in the outer world for similar repair.

WEEK 2: AUGUST 10–16, 2020

The Moon moves through Taurus, Gemini, and Cancer this week. Once the Moon gets to Cancer, she begins to oppose the major planets in Capricorn, triggering emotions. The major transits of the week are Mercury square Uranus and Mars square Pluto.

Mercury squares (challenges) Uranus this week. Nerves may be on edge and the pace of the week is fast. Energies are running high. You can get a lot done but do be prepared for possible surprises and setbacks. The best path is to go with the flow.

Later in the week, Mars in Aries squares (challenges) Pluto in Capricorn. The high side of this transit is the ability to creatively transform the world, and the lowest expression would be disagreements and power struggles. Primarily this plays out in the energy of the individual versus the energy of groups. Try to stay above the fray, but do not fear standing up for or supporting a cause near and dear to you.

Shadow: Reaction. This week shows us the potential for changing the world from the inside out. It's time to reach for something higher. However, your instinct may be to first seek change through reaction, and that means you can miss the true choice in your actions. Practice responding not reacting. Breathe deep before "doing". Take a reflective pause before striking out or saying something that can't be undone later.

Week 3: August 17–23, 2020

This is the week of the New Moon in Leo, but before starting something new, clarify what your heart's desires are. The rest of the week is an easy flow, yet the background of energies that have been in play are still there and you may still be dealing with them.

Monday before the New Moon is a little intense with Mercury conjunct the Sun and trining Mars. Stay present, aware, and in your body. The three of these planets work together to bring lots to do, many conversations to have, and the potential for accidents and missteps if you're moving too fast.

The New Moon in Leo is the last major configuration for the week. See August Moons below.

On Saturday, the Sun moves into Virgo. You may be more organic in your approach to dealing with issues of health, work, and taking care of the details. It is a time of preparing for the eventual onset of winter. In the process, you can neaten up your life and become more practical and organized. Clean out closets, Feng Shui your home or office, and reduce-reuse-recycle.

Shadow: Turbulence and the dark night of the collective soul. These are powerful times and we are all being asked to rise to the occasion through embracing our divinity. In 2019, we gained the spiritual chops to move through anything. Remember this when the world turns chaotic, stay tuned in to what spirituality means to you.

Week 4: August 24–30, 2020

Warning: Crazy week ahead! Mars heads into a challenge with Saturn on Monday. Tuesday it's Mercury, Uranus, Venus, and Jupiter in positive aspect to one another. Wednesday is a bit calmer; Thursday is spiritual salve for us through Venus and Neptune. Friday and Saturday, the Moon in Capricorn triggers Jupiter, Pluto, and Saturn and challenges Mars. On Sunday, Venus opposes powerful Pluto while Mercury opposes spiritual Neptune.

Even if you're not that familiar with astrology, you can sense that this is going to be a packed week. It's not that this is a bad week, just one that is likely going to keep you off balance a bit. Handle this week with patience, lots of deep breathing, and a dose of humor.

Around August 24, military action of some kind cannot be ruled out. Mars rules war and military action while Saturn rules the military as an institution. Does this mean a false flag operation of some kind? A terrorist event? Or a military invasion? The truth of any military action may be hard to come by. Stay open-minded, be prepared, and don't move in to fear.

Shadow: Constriction. In the face of so much going on in the world and in your personal life, you may feel like love has all but left the planet. You may physiologically be constricting your own breathing as you anticipate and prepare for things that have yet to happen. This causes needless suffering. Remember the Serenity Prayer and the line about acceptance: *God grant me the serenity to accept the things I cannot change, the courage to change the things I can, and the wisdom to know the difference.*

··

August Moons

FULL MOON @ 12° AQUARIUS | AUGUST 3, AT 11:59 AM ET

MOON MUSINGS:

Make way for the new and the innovative by releasing the old and outdated. The Moon and Uranus form a challenging aspect now, but it gives you the emotional edge to try new things, to experiment, to dream of what might be.

With Mercury opposing Saturn during this Moon cycle, there is strong encouragement to take the best of your traditions and your past with you on the journey into the future. Some may find this Full Moon exciting and others may not be ready to move forward into the new. Either way, don't "throw the baby out with the bathwater." Release what is not sustainable or serving you and embrace the innovative and unique.

NEW MOON @ 26° LEO | AUGUST 18, AT 10:42 PM ET

MOON MUSINGS:

A time of renewed confidence, generosity, and open-heartedness is your potential creative push this month. Leo New Moons remind us that our heart's desires are only one conscious step away. Get a clear picture of what it is you want to create in your life, then dare to take a step toward it. The only thing that would hold you back is a lack of confidence.

Earth and Fire energy dominate this New Moon. Earth is grounding and gives us access to the practical steps we need to create, and fire is the energy of passion and creativity. In the chart for this New Moon, the planets form what looks like a kite. A kite configuration is filled with potential and the smooth flow of energy. Take advantage!

There are still the Mars squares to Jupiter, Pluto, and Saturn to contend with, but these are consistent energies at play for the next few months. They may be fueling the potential for what we want to create. So even though there may be upsets still going on in the background, it does not need to stop you from personally being creative.

Resources

NUMEROLOGY: 3 UNIVERSAL MONTH IN A 4 UNIVERSAL YEAR

KEY WORDS: SOCIALIZE, DETAILS, EXPRESSION

Nap time is officially over. August will have you back in the saddle again. This is a 3 universal month which will be far more social than last month. Your energy is back and it's a great time to start new social circles. Maybe you are hoping to expand your social life. The 4 universal year provides a healthy dose of "attention to detail" while the 3 allows you to be the unpredictable social butterfly. If you are interested in getting support for some kind of volunteer effort, this is perfect for rallying the troops. You will have a natural flair for expressing exactly what you need so that you can get the job done. This energy is also great for event planning. Are you thinking of building? The combined vibration of the 3 and the 4 say it's a super time to start talking about your plans for the future. Whether it involves talking to a contractor or a financial planner, the energy lends itself to talking with those who can help you execute your plan.

GEMSTONE WISDOM: POLISHED MALACHITE

Happy dance! Polished Malachite helps to enhance your 'social butterfly' energy (even for us introverts) and be more open to social gatherings. It lessens shyness and is a great supporter of friendships. Use the expressive energy of Malachite to share your feelings and be open-minded to new opportunities.

ESSENTIAL OIL APPLICATION:

The oils offered this month align with the themes of detail and expression. The Virgo energies are all about details, details, details. Are you a pro at the details? Not so much? Some of the most interesting benefits of essential oils are their ability to activate feelings or attributes that may be dormant. Let the oils do what they do best this month and enhance the diligent awareness of the details, Lighting up ideas and next steps that are ready to take flight. Along with doing this work, you may also feel a need to express these thoughts either verbally or creatively. Express away and know that, in doing so, you open yourself up to the rewards "being in the flow" can bring you.

- **Rosemary -** Place 1-2 drops on back of neck near base of skull. Cup hands and breathe in remaining oil from hands with eyes closed. Place 2 drops in a diffuser whenever you want to enhance the details of your day. Rosemary can support retaining the information you see, read, and hear. Offering perspective to the details and information you take in, Rosemary can clear away the unnecessary input you are taking in and decide what is helpful to hold on to.

- **Inspiring Blend -** A blend of Cardamom, Cinnamon, Ginger, Clove, Sandalwood, Jasmine Absolute, and Damiana leaf. Apply 1-2 drops of this blend on heart/chest area, behind ears, or on wrists. This blend may activate your newest inspirational idea that is ready to be born. Promotes feelings of passionate creativity, in whatever form it is uniquely expressed through you.

Chakras supported by these oils: Brow Throat, Heart, Solar Plexus, Root

POSITIVE AFFIRMATION/INTENTION:
Everything I need to see presents itself to me exactly when I need it. I allow my natural expression to be revealed.

MOVEMENT OF THE MONTH: SEATED TWIST

August is a good time for clearing out and creating space for open-mindedness and happiness. This month's energy reflects the benefits of cleaning out while getting clear in our thoughts and environment. Start by adding Marichyasana III, or gentle seated twists, to your practice. This is a wringing out pose which releases toxins and replenishes the organs with fresh blood flow.

Seated on the floor, extend your left leg. Pull right leg up so knee is bent and right foot is on floor, placing right foot beside your left knee. Push out through the ball of the foot on the extended leg, (illustration is shown with a bent knee variation) have toes pointed upward. Inhale as your right arm lifts up and over your head, rotating it backward to place your palm on the floor behind your right buttocks, supporting an elongated spine. Bring your left hand to your right knee and exhale as you rotate your left ribs toward your right ribs. Creating a wringing motion with your torso starting at your spine and rotating upwards, neck and head last. Continuing to inhale and revolve or hold on the exhale for 3 breaths. Gently release on the last exhale, unwinding from the tailbone, shoulders, head and neck last. Repeat on the other side. Twisting and revolving postures allow for a gentle squeezing and replenishing of our internal organs, letting go and releasing, and creating space for health and wellness.

NOURISHMENT :

Things get really rough this month. Spiritual and nourishment practices need to be on point because even when they are, you can still find yourself saying, "Jesus, Take the Wheel!" I'm not trying to promote eating cookies or drinking wine… but certainly there are days and times for those… but for this segment, it's that NONE of that will work… and that it's time to get on your knees. It's hard to focus and the anxiety is so high that meditation feels miles away. This is where the Serenity Prayer comes into play. Take some deep breaths and say it over and over again until you feel a shift.

"God,
Grant me the serenity…
to accept the things I cannot change,
the courage to change the things I can,
and the wisdom to know the difference. "

It's important to be mindful of sweets during late summer. A little bit goes a long way. Sugar is everywhere and ice-cream for dinner happens. This is the season to nourish your stomach (more on gut health next moon cycle) and spleen/pancreas, so be mindful not to over tax these systems by reaching for refined sugar and processed carbs to dull the edges.

THE HEALTHY GODMOTHER HINT: Healthy fats like coconut oil are great at calming the central nervous system as well as balancing blood sugar levels. Coconut oil also acts as an anti-inflammatory, supports proper gut balance, and aids in lining the myelin sheaths in the brain which calms your nerves and supports function and focus. Use it while sautéing greens, add a chunk to your smoothies or blended coffee, or when things get really rugged, eat it with a spoon like your favorite nut butter.

FOODS THAT NOURISH:
- Everything at the farmers' market
- Nuts & Seeds
- Ice cream

SEASONAL FOCUS:
- Season of late summer
- Nourishing the stomach and spleen

CHAKRAS AT PLAY: Throat & Sacral

RECIPES:
- Cranberry Flush Pops
- Protein Bites

JOURNAL THIS:

WHAT IN MY LIFE IS GENERATIVE AND CREATIVE? WHAT IS POSSIBLE FOR ME THAT I HAVEN'T EVEN CONSIDERED?

Love this information? Get your own private reading or consultation by visiting the writers' personal websites which can be found in the back of The Energy Almanac.

August Notes

September

CHOICE. MAGIC. FOCUS. GRATITUDE.

AUGUST 31–SEPTEMBER 6

Do listen for empowering messages.

Don't stay victim or martyr.

SEPTEMBER 7–13

Do walk your talk.

Don't take everything from your past into your future.

SEPTEMBER 14–20

Do step into your personal power.

Don't overthink.

SEPTEMBER 21–27

Do observe from a place of love.

Don't hold onto old stories and current drama.

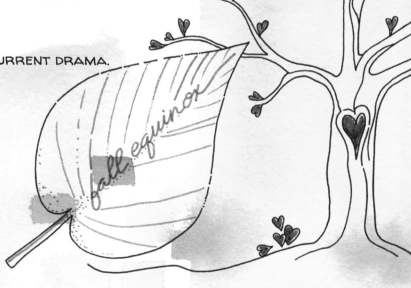

SEPTEMBER 2

FULL MOON IN PISCES

Watch for deception and confusion.

SEPTEMBER 17

NEW MOON IN VIRGO

High level discernment.

Energy Almanac 2020 Edition

 ✩ www.shopBigSky.com ✩

September

CHOICE. MAGIC. FOCUS. GRATITUDE.

Thank you, thank you, thank you! Rely on the energy of Tigers Eye to focus on what you want and release all that is holding you back. Allow the magic of creativity to surround you and be grateful for all you receive. Ask the Universe to "bring it" and be open to the wonder.

DATES TO WATCH:

- **September 1-2, Full Moon in Pisces.** See September Moons below.

- **September 5, Mercury into Libra.** Are you saying what you think people want to hear? The potential is for diplomatic, tactful, and peaceful conversations.

- **September 6, Venus into Leo.** Love and romance take center stage in your personal life.

- **September 9, Mars turns retrograde in Aries.** Action and forward momentum is stalled, causing frustration.

- **September 12, Jupiter turns direct in Capricorn.** Ethics, solutions, and resourcefulness in the news again.

- **September 17, New Moon in Virgo.** See September Moons below.

- **September 22, Sun into Libra and Autumn/Spring equinox.** Time for the three C's - collaboration, co-creation, and cooperation. Relationships come into focus.

- **September 27, Mercury into Scorpio.** Communication tinged with passion and intensity. The mind goes deep.

ASTROLOGY BY THE WEEKS:

WEEK 1: AUGUST 31 – SEPTEMBER 6. 2020
Full Moon in Pisces, Mercury connects with Pluto and Saturn, Venus opposes Pluto, Mercury moves into Libra, Venus moves into Leo.

We start the week with the Full Moon in Pisces. The high potential for everyone is to wake up and snap out of codependent confusion and step into idealistic creativity. This is a Full Moon of victim-martyr type energy. If you're playing either side, it's time to become empowered. See September Moons below.

This week also portends a profound shift in the speech and messages we are hearing. Mercury trines (flows nicely) with Pluto, and Saturn is spreading an empowering message. Make a list for how you can practically and organically move ahead. In the United States, we are still in the election cycle, and this may be the start of a more precise message from candidates.

Venus opposing Saturn and the Sun in trine with Uranus on Wednesday have us searching for truth and impeccability. Do you even know truth when it is staring you in the face or do you rationalize away what is obviously untrue? Until we demand more of ourselves, we won't see those characteristics of truth and impeccability in the outer world.

Mercury and Venus end the week by moving into the new signs of Mercury into Libra (where you can explore truth through tact and diplomacy or indecision and superficiality), and Venus into Leo (where you explore what constitutes love and self-centeredness versus greed and narcissism).

Shadow: Blame is victim energy. Any time you set out to blame others, the outer world, or heritage, you are engaging in victim or martyr energy. To be healthy in this world, one has to lay claim to truth and integrity, which can only come when you claim responsibility for yourself and your creations. The Full Moon this week helped us see where we may still be playing the role of victim in our lives so we can illuminate, release, and transform that energy.

WEEK 2: SEPTEMBER 7–13, 2020
This week the Sun trines Jupiter, Mars turns retrograde in Aries, the Sun opposes Neptune from Virgo to Pisces, and Jupiter turns direct in Capricorn.

There is a mix of subtle and overt energies this week. The Sun trines Jupiter in retrograde, illuminating the next steps in your personal evolution of consciousness. The same day, Mars turns retrograde in his own sign of Aries, giving us an extended period of possible passive-aggressive energy and frustration. Or does Mars retrograde slow us down so we can consider just what direction we really want to move in? It all depends on your view of what's happening in the world around you.

The Sun opposes Neptune this week to remind you that you are not just physical/ego bodies, but also spiritual and soul-oriented. The Sun shines its light in places where you have deluded yourself or where you just haven't seen yourself in holistic terms yet.

Ending the week is Jupiter moving forward once more in the sign of Capricorn. While retrograde, Jupiter has been pushing you to consider where you may be stuck in the past or hesitant to let go of the old. Why not blend the best of the past with the most hopeful and forward-looking future? Consider that over the next couple of months before Jupiter moves us into Aquarius.

Shadow: Be aware of wolves in sheep's clothing. Demand transparency and ethics of yourself and others. Peer beneath the surface of words you are hearing or speaking and the motives of the people saying them (or your own). Consider what filters you are viewing the world through.

WEEK 3: SEPTEMBER 14–20, 2020
Warning: Busy week ahead! There is a powerful Sun trine Pluto, then Venus squares Uranus. There is a high energy New Moon in Virgo with Mercury in Libra beginning to challenge the planets in Capricorn (Jupiter, Pluto, Saturn). Events may have your head spinning, or you've become immune to the potency of what is going on.

On display either in your personal life or in the world around you are both power struggles and empowerment. The Sun and Pluto in a trine suggest that we are becoming more personally powerful, and yet, that is usually born out of our personal struggles to become empowered or to take power away from others. Take time to consider the effects of power vs. powerlessness in your life.

The New Moon is highly energetic and involves many connections with planets. See September Moons below.

Mercury in Libra, teaching us about tact, diplomacy, and the value of creating win-win situations, is now beginning to challenge the planets in Capricorn to "walk their talk." You, as an individual, are also tasked with the same.

Shadow: Confusion, oppression, hopelessness. The three of these energies are tied to mental anxiety or over thinking. Be ever diligent to not allow your mind to overtake your heart. It is one of the biggest lessons we are learning now. The crazy outer world is only a "picture" of the shadow our minds have created. It is time to let go of dependence on the mind and go deeper into the heart and emotions. Relaxing the mind allows us to realize the truth.

WEEK 4: SEPTEMBER 21–27, 2020
We pass through the Autumn/Spring Equinox this week. Mercury finishes triggering the Capricorn triple conjunction of Jupiter, Pluto, and Saturn while the Moon in Capricorn conjuncts them. The week ends with Mercury moving into Scorpio.

Looking at the chart for the Autumn/Spring equinox shows that we are grappling mightily with whether we move forward or we hold on to the traditions and old ideals of who we are in the world. This is why Rome fell. It couldn't hold on to its past glory and still be a force for leadership in the future. Is the USA doomed to repeat the mistakes of Rome? That is the choice point we find ourselves at now. Do we hold onto the old concept of power and might that created a USA super power? Or can we make the transition to being leaders for the future of the world? Likewise, in your personal chart, where are you holding on to past glories and not transitioning into a new reality?

Really listen to the messages of the people around you now. What are you hearing? Is it positive and uplifting or is it the same old message of division and polarization? Use what you're hearing as an access point to your own consciousness. What do you want to create? The emotional tone is volatile right now. Be drawn into the drama or rise above and choose a higher path.

Shadow: Constriction and seriousness. We are either in the shadow of constriction and seriousness, or we use love and end up in acceptance and delight. What we choose now we will be facing for the foreseeable future.

September Moons

FULL MOON @ 10° PISCES | SEPTEMBER 2, AT 1:23 AM ET

MOON MUSINGS:
The chart for the Full Moon in Pisces is a bit of a mess with planets spread around the whole of the chart. This means there is a lot going on, and it might be difficult for you to be clear about your role in the world in the face of so much activity.

First step to clarity is to choose love, compassion, and the recognition of our shared values, and release the cacophony of voices raised in separation. There may be false voices raised in this Full Moon. Pisces energy can be deceptive. Don't fall prey to the words of people whose deeds do not match their words. Be very discerning now.

The Sun and Moon each make many minor connections to planets now. These influences might feel like bees buzzing around, or the irritations of too many things going on at once. Move into your spiritual practices to help you get through these days. Favor listening with your heart over the confusion created by the mind. Use your intuition. Be discerning. See through the falsehoods.

NEW MOON @ 25° VIRGO | SEPTEMBER 17, AT 7:00 AM ET

MOON MUSINGS:
Virgo in its highest form is discerning and healing. The highest potential of this New Moon then, is your being able to use discernment in the choices you make in intentions and manifestations.

The degree of this New Moon also holds keys to what is possible. Dane Rudhyar in his book, "An Astrological Mandala: The Cycle of Transformations and Its 360 Symbolic Phases" highlights this degree of Virgo as, "The first stage of actual participation in the great ritual of planetary evolution." YES! And the good news is we are conscious participants in this ritual. If you could create the world of your dreams, highest hopes, and aspirations, what would it look like? These are the potent places to put your attention. Never mind the petty sniping, quarrels, and divisions you are seeing around you. This is the first sign of the magic we hold to change the world!

. . . .

Resources

NUMEROLOGY: 4 UNIVERSAL MONTH IN A 4 UNIVERSAL YEAR

KEY WORDS: MAGIC, FOCUS, GRATITUDE

Wowzers! This promises to be a very intense month. September is a 4-universal month in a 4-universal year. Be very careful where you place your focus this month. This is almost a magical vibration that says anything you give your energy, attention, and focus to will get bigger. The 4 vibration reminds us to focus on the details. It typically brings in a lot of work-related experiences. The 4 is a foundational year but if you focus on how many bricks you don't have to build your foundation with, you'll be plagued with never having enough bricks. On the other hand, if you focus on celebrating how many bricks you DO have, you'll attract more bricks. This month, make sure you approach everything with a healthy dose of gratitude, including the obstacles, so they can cease being a problem. Choose to focus on what is right rather than what is wrong.

GEMSTONE WISDOM: TIGERS EYE

Rely on the energy of Tigers Eye to focus on what you want and release all that is holding you back. Allow the magic of creativity to surround you and be grateful for all you receive. Ask the Universe to "bring it" and be open to the wonder.

ESSENTIAL OIL APPLICATION:

September kicks us off with some magic, focus, and gratitude vibes. Let's take full advantage of these key areas. To keep up with the pace of what September is forecasting, you would benefit from clarity and focus. Choose oils that guide you toward clarity, so that you may shine a light on areas in your life you are working to enhance. Invite magical outcomes, expect miracles. Sometimes all that is needed is a gentle reminder that you have limitless potential. Consider this your reminder, my friend. It is time to claim that potential and hold gratitude that everything works out as it should.

- **Spikenard -** Apply 1 drop over heart. You may also wish to apply 2 drops to the bottom of each foot. Spikenard, with its very distinct earthy aroma is the most effective oil to generate and allow feelings of gratitude. Experiencing gratitude is unmistakable in its warm wave that washes over the soul. Pure in its form, gratitude and love go hand in hand. Start and end your day with spikenard. Incorporating it into your daily morning and evening routine can result in profound effects.

- **Lemon -** Diffuse 3 drops in an essential oil diffuser. Apply 1-2 drops in palm of hands, close eyes, and breathe in deeply when you are feeling like you need additional focus. Add 10 drops of lemon to a spray bottle with water and spray in the air. The fresh crisp scent of lemon is incredibly uplifting and has great impact on mental focus and concentration. When energy levels in the body are low, lemon can reignite the drive within, quiet insecurities, and bring a sense of joy back to your being.

Chakras supported by these oils: Crown, Throat, Solar Plexus, Root

POSITIVE AFFIRMATION/INTENTION:
I embrace gratitude with ease. Clarity is abundant for me now.

MOVEMENT OF THE MONTH: TREE POSE

September's energies are about releasing confusion, rooting down, listening with your heart, and listening to your intuition for focused growth and expansion while being mindful and conservative. Add Vrksasana Tree Pose to your daily practice now. Being flexible to bend in the breeze helps you to stay strong and not become uprooted.

Tree Pose assists with practicing balance and focus on and off the mat. Starting in Mountain Pose, shift your balance to one foot before dropping the tailbone down. Inhale. Bring the sole of one foot to the calf or inner thigh of the opposite leg. (Never place your foot at your knee as it's a moveable joint.) Exhale and extend your arms upward with palms a few inches apart facing each other. Extend the index fingers. Drop the tailbone, rooting in the foot, and let your eyes find a non-moving object no more than 12 inches from the floor. This is your focal point to concentrate on. Find balance, strength, and harmony as a tree in nature. Have fun with it and enjoy the freshness of balance, clarity, and space.

NOURISHMENT:

As we go from late summer into fall, you will continue to be asked to "stomach" a lot of change, conflict, and emotional turmoil. This year has been a lot to "digest", and it's beyond important that your gut, the receiver of nourishment, is functioning at its optimal level. The easiest thing you can do to support your digestion is to chew your food more. Be mindful of meal times. Sit down. Light a candle. Say grace. Breathe. Our bodies don't digest when stressed, and when you're mindlessly eating or eating while on the run, things begin to back up on you causing gas, bloating, and acid reflux. Slow down and give your gut a hand by chewing your food until it's liquid before swallowing. It makes a huge difference. Incorporating quality probiotics, digestive enzymes, and fermented veggies (cabbage, onions, peppers), and kimchi will also help you process and assimilate all that is being served up on the "buffets" in your life right now.

THE HEALTHY GODMOTHER HINT: Once you are digesting and assimilating things more easily, practice speaking from the heart and support the chakras at play this month.

Say what you mean,
mean what you say,
but don't say it mean.

FOODS THAT NOURISH:
- Farmers' Market Finds
- Eat the rainbow
- Apples
- Squashes

SEASONAL FOCUS:
- Gut health - Chew your food
- Prepping, canning, freezing

CHAKRAS AT PLAY: Throat and heart

RECIPES:
- Grain-Free Apple Crisp
- #betterthan Chia Chai Lattes
- The Art of Sacred Eating
- Fermented Veggies

JOURNAL THIS:

WHAT HAVE I DECIDED IS CRAZY THAT IS ACTUALLY POSSIBLE? WHAT MAGIC CAN I BE AND RECEIVE TODAY/THIS MONTH/THIS YEAR?

Love this information? Get your own private reading or consultation by visiting the writers' personal websites which can be found in the back of The Energy Almanac.

September Notes

October

PERSPECTIVE. PLAY. WORK. BALANCE

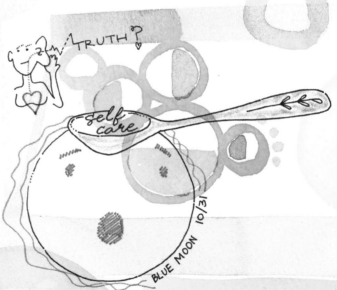

SEPTEMBER 28–OCTOBER 4

Do prune away at old thinking.
Don't be judgemental of yourself or others.

OCTOBER 5–11

Do consider how you can show up differently in life.
Don't be so stubborn.

OCTOBER 12–18

Do listen with your heart.
Don't fear the future.

OCTOBER 19–25

Do practice self-care.
Don't quit too soon; stay the course.

OCTOBER 26–NOVEMBER 1

Do stay open-minded to surprise revelations. Don't avoid change; notice where you are stuck.

OCTOBER 1
FULL MOON IN ARIES
Confronting the shadow.

OCTOBER 16
NEW MOON SUPERMOON IN LIBRA
Life changing transformation.

OCTOBER 31
BLUE MOON–FULL MOON IN TAURUS
A rebellious awakening.

☆ www.shopBigSky.com ☆

October

PERSPECTIVE. PLAY. WORK. BALANCE.

October presents us with the next level of all the transits we have been experiencing since June, with the additional energy for releasing and letting go in new realities.

October has two Full Moons and a super New Moon in Libra. The second Full Moon of October falls right on Halloween and is accompanied by a Sun opposing Uranus transit. It feels like a fall from grace for someone prominent in the world. Someone or something being exposed to the light and there is a relative awakening because of it.

With Mars in Aries and the Sun in Libra, there are plenty of opportunities for challenges to work through, and you have the tools to do the work required. That doesn't mean it feels good, but that could just be your perspective. Change the way you look at things and the things you're looking at change. That might be a great mantra for October and indeed the rest of 2020!

DATES TO WATCH:

- **September 28, Saturn turns direct.** Karma, comeuppance, authoritarianism exposed.

- **September 29, Mars retrograde squares Saturn.** Go back to August 24 to reread what was written about possible military actions. Mars is going back over the same degree it did back on that date.

- **October 1, Full Moon in Aries.** See October Moons below.

- **October 2, Venus into Virgo.** Values, finances, and love interests turn practical. Watch out for pickiness and perfectionism in your relationships.

- **October 4, Pluto turns direct.** Release and flush.

- **October 13, Mercury turns retrograde in Scorpio.** Seeking the truth in the hidden. Intuitively connecting with what isn't being said.

- **October 16, New Moon - Super Moon in Libra.** See October Moons below.

- **October 22, Sun into Scorpio.** Healing and transforming energy that also seeks to expose the hidden, dark, or undercurrents of what is happening.

- **October 27, Mercury retrogrades back into Libra and Venus into Libra.** Balancing and harmonizing.

Energy Almanac 2020 Edition

- **October 31, Halloween, Blue Moon, Full Moon in Taurus.** See October Moons below.

- **October 31, Sun in Scorpio opposes Uranus in Taurus.** Identity, ego, power and pride in individuals resulting in conflict and a fall from grace.

ASTROLOGY BY THE WEEKS:

WEEK 1: SEPTEMBER 28 – OCTOBER 4, 2020
This first week of October brings Saturn in late Capricorn returning to forward motion and a cantankerous Full Moon in Aries.

Saturn has been retrograde since May. He now turns direct to finish up his 3-year sojourn of Capricorn. We are in the last of Saturn's restructure and reforming of our lives and of the world. The job isn't totally complete yet; there is still opportunity to prune your life down to what is really important to you and let go of anything that isn't authentic anymore. Claim your authority, be authentic, and set your sights on expressing the true you.

The Full Moon in Aries this week is also a highly energetic series of transits. The Moon energy holds a lot of potential for a more spiritual connection in all we do. (See October Moons below.)

Shadow: Judgment and being judgmental. The biggest shadow is you projecting your own fear of being "not good enough" out into the world. To release the fear, find your personal integrity and discover how perfect you are in the moment. This week also holds another interesting shadow energy in the idea of patriarchy. This feels like a turning point in the rebalancing of the masculine and feminine on the planet.

WEEK 2: OCTOBER 5–11, 2020
Mercury opposes Uranus, Mars squares Pluto, Venus trines Uranus, and the Sun challenges Jupiter.

Even with several transits this week, it doesn't feel too challenging or overly dramatic. It does feel like we are having an eye-opening discussion, which opens our minds to what is possible and exposes the fears that have us seeking security and protection.

Mercury opposing Uranus causes us to question all our sacred cows. Mars squaring Pluto shows you what to transform and how to end fighting and conflict. Venus trine Uranus invites you to try new things, and act in new ways with one another. The Sun and Jupiter may show you what you are stubbornly holding onto that no longer serves. Be willing to transform, to see things differently, and to entertain new ideas and possibilities this week.

Shadow: The shadow of inadequacy means always questioning whether you know enough, have enough credentials, or are worthy enough to demonstrate your skills in the world. Giving in to this shadow holds you back and stops you from achieving mastery in your life. Instead, connect to your inner resources that are always available: intuition, knowing, and instinct.

Energy Almanac **2020 Edition**

Week 3: October 12–18, 2020

There is a New Moon this week which is also a Super Moon (meaning the Moon comes to within 90% of the closest approach it can make to Earth). The "super" status of the Moon charges it up and gives it substantial power to affect change and new beginnings.

Everything about this week is the lead up to the New Moon in Libra. The Libra New Moon challenges us to seek new beginnings of harmony, equilibrium, equality, diplomacy, and balance. This is often splashed across the political scene, and here in the USA we are just 3 weeks shy of the presidential election. You can bet there is a lot of talk, conflict, and disharmony.

The Sun opposes Mars and squares Pluto this week. There is still potential for some military action or confrontation. Peace and prosperity based in equality is the goal. There are strong voices and opinions out there this week. Can you find your way to your heart with all the rhetoric? It's important that we find the heart-centered path through these trying times.

Shadow: Fear of the future or unease about what is to come. There are a lot of distracting events, people, and talk out there, possibly triggering fear in you. Here's the good news: you have an inborn sensibility that helps you ascertain the truth. You can recognize hidden agendas, sense the true vibration of the people around you, and tune in to what truth sounds like.

Week 4: October 19–25, 2020

This week the Moon moves through Capricorn in conjunction with Jupiter, Pluto, and Saturn (our triple conjunction). Venus trines Pluto and Saturn, the Sun moves into Scorpio and Mercury retrograde conjuncts the Sun in Scorpio.

Expect this to be an emotional week as people are triggered by the Moon moving through an area of our charts populated by many planets. Many are experiencing emotional burnout. Practice self-care, self-nurturing, self-love, and compassion if you are feeling emotional upset. Take a break from the news and your technology and get out into nature for calming relief.

Mercury retrograde conjuncts the Sun in Scorpio. Reconnect to your passions and what makes you feel alive. Along with Venus working easily with Pluto and Saturn this week, this helps you gain clarity and insight into how you want to move forward.

Shadow: Fear of failure or fear of success? When you're afraid of failure you may stop yourself before you reach success or use the fear as an excuse to not move forward. Either way, it is a negative expression. Try to hold a steady course. If you are passionate or love what you're doing, don't give up before you hit success. Also consider if deep within you might be the fear of what comes next if all your dreams come true. Interesting to consider, isn't it?

Week 5: October 26–November 1, 2020

There is a Blue Moon, Full Moon in Taurus this week on Halloween. The Sun is opposing Uranus during the Full Moon which means surprises, revolution, and revelations.

The biggest news of the week is the second Full Moon, or Blue Moon, in Taurus. The Moon will be conjunct Uranus and that puts the Sun in an opposition to Uranus. Expect to be surprised by something or someone. There may also be epiphanies that lead you through a problem you've grappled with. Stay open-minded.

Shadow: Fear of failing in your responsibilities to your family or community. Fear like this causes you to give too much of yourself and then working from a deficit instead of from bounty. Look deeply into why you may be doing what you're doing. You may discover that nurturing yourself as well as your family/friends/co-workers/community is far more fulfilling than you expected.

....

October Moons

FULL MOON @ 9° ARIES | OCTOBER 1, AT 5:06 PM ET

MOON MUSINGS:

The Full Moon is a time of releasing, completion, and even revelation as the full light of the Moon shines into our lives and charts. The Moon and Sun are across from one another in Libra/Aries and that brings relationships into focus. Relationships are really the mirrors of what we ourselves need to learn most. If you have a difficult relationship with someone, this is a call for you to look deeply into the mirror and see what the relationship really means for you. This can be hugely healing as you realize the other person is simply showing you where you yourself are out of balance or harmony with yourself.

Since the Moon is in Aries now and also conjunct Chiron (the wounded healer), there is the possibility of having to confront your own shadow or help someone else who is confronting their own shadow. Healing with this Moon requires releasing co-dependence and embracing interdependence. The true lesson here is that we are all together in this life and need one another at times.

NEW MOON—SUPER MOON @ 24° LIBRA | OCTOBER 16, AT 3:32 PM ET

MOON MUSINGS:

A Super Moon happens when the Moon comes to within 90% of the closest approach it ever makes to us on Earth. A Super Moon can occur at the new phase or at the full phase. Whichever phase it happens in, we are capable of running more energy through our systems. In this case, we're supercharged with potential creative energy.

This Moon has the Sun and Moon conjunct in an opposition to Mars and in a square to Pluto. It is literally a life-changing and life-transforming New Moon. Now is the time to choose new beginnings that nurture and bring stability to our lives. There are many other configurations that are supporting us to make the necessary changes to be who we want to be. Don't let this Moon go by without setting some powerful intentions.

HALLOWEEN BLUE MOON–FULL MOON @ 9° TAURUS | OCTOBER 31, AT 10:49 AM ET

MOON MUSINGS:

The second Full Moon in one calendar month is called a Blue Moon, and this month we are graced with another opportunity to release, complete, and move on. This is a surprise driven Full Moon as the Moon conjuncts Uranus and the Sun opposes it.

Uranus is the rebel awakener. He shows us plainly where we have stagnated and then invites us to change. If you choose to change, all is good. But if you stay stuck, you become increasingly more frustrated and self-defeating. On a subconscious level, the energy of Uranus then creates a possible trauma or drama to make you move. Your opportunity then is to look deeply into your life, see where you are stuck, and choose to release and move forward.

Resources

NUMEROLOGY: 5 UNIVERSAL MONTH IN A 4 UNIVERSAL YEAR

KEY WORDS: PLAY, WORK, BALANCE

Here comes another month full of contradictions. This month will be similar to January where the 5 universal month will be asking us to come out to play but the 4 universal year resists the invitation by saying, "NO! I have to work." Any time we see 5 energy, we need to be reminded to not squander our energy aimlessly. The 5 is all about living life to the fullest but the 4 says, "Not without a plan, you don't!" Remember that kid in school who resisted being a rebel? He never wanted to risk getting into trouble, but one day he decided to skip school and his life was forever changed. He took a risk and loved it. He didn't get caught. He had fun and still had time to ace his homework later. This is what the 5 universal month in a 4 universal year can feel like. The 5 invites fun, but remember to resist scattering your energy all over the place. You can enjoy change with some healthy "4" boundaries in place. This can be an amazing blend of energies if you learn to balance the need for your freedom with the need for a plan.

GEMSTONE WISDOM: EMERALD

Do I, or don't I? Work-life balance is the constant questioning and evaluating of priorities. The good news is that the steady and balancing energy of Emerald brings to light the positive aspects of life. This gemstone encourages living life to the fullest and stabilizing you mentally, emotionally, and physically. Emerald embodies integrity and loyalty and fosters cooperation.

ESSENTIAL OIL APPLICATION:

October shows us there is an urge for play and work balance. When you feel out of sorts, one of the best ways to bring your body back into balance is by utilizing the gifts this earth has given you. When fearful uncertain thoughts or feelings rise up within you, honor and thank them, but let them know they're not invited to stay. This month's oils can assure your inner child that he/she is safe. You are reminded that your thoughts are powerful creations of your daily experience. Use these oils to promote feelings of security and confidence, which can leave you feeling lighter and more hopeful for your future.

- **Green Mandarin -** (topical use dilute with carrier oil) Place 3 drops in a diffuser. Apply 2 drops over heart and 1 drop on wrists. Some people work hard, others play hard. When the scales of this balance have been tipped, Green Mandarin invites you to find harmony in these areas. A healthy dose of fun and pleasantly uplifting, this oil can be supportive in reducing fear and self-doubt, returning you back to a lighter state of being.

- **Steadying Blend -** A blend of Lavender, Cedarwood, Frankincense, Cinnamon Bark, Sandalwood, Black Pepper, and Patchouli. Apply 2 drops to lower back (sacrum). Apply 2 drops to the bottom of each foot. Steadying Blend encourages balance and being grounded in the body. Lessening fear and apprehension as you walk on your path, this supportive combination oil can keep you putting one foot in front of the other as you trek your way through uncertainty. Bravely walk forward in your strength.

Chakras supported by these oils: Crown, Brow, Throat, Solar Plexus, Sacral, Root

POSITIVE AFFIRMATION/INTENTION:
The courage to move forward is within me. I am enough.

MOVEMENT OF THE MONTH: MIGHTY POWERFUL POSE

This month seek inner power by adding Ukatasana, or Mighty Powerful Pose, to your daily routine. "Change the way you look at things and the things you're looking at change," is the mantra for October. Root down in your heels. Inhale with your arms extending overhead and palms together, interlocking fingers with index fingers pointing upwards. Exhale, bending the knees and engaging your leg muscles. Drop the tailbone down as if lowering into a chair. The energy within us rises from the navel through the tips of the fingers, igniting our life force. Take several breaths to deepen the pose or hold, creating heat and vitality while keeping in your mind's eye your positive intention for the future. Visualize light energy flowing out of your feet, through your fingertips, and out the crown of your head. Breathe slowly, listen with your heart, awaken to your divine truth, and embrace your soul's essence. Take 3-5 breaths here. As you release out of the pose, pause in Mountain Pose, inhale and exhale slowly, visualizing what you want to manifest in your life.

NOURISHMENT:

With the season of fall and all the shedding that we're being asked to do in terms of embracing new ways and releasing the old, it's time for a cleanse. Where have you been with your 80/20 rule? Again, wherever you are is perfect; just slide closer to the 80/20 or 90/10. Support your efforts with some spaghetti squash and meatballs (or meat sauce) with lots of fresh basil and nutritional yeast, or tacos with lots of fresh cilantro in your pineapple mango salsa*.

You can also cleanse from the outside in with an apple cider vinegar(ACV) and epsom salt bath. The magnesium in the epsom serves as an amazing muscle relaxant, and the salts and vinegar draw toxins. If baths aren't your thing, you can fill a spray bottle with the ingredients and leave in your shower for a daily spritz. Once you try an ACV Spritzer* you won't be able to live without it.

Shoulders down. Unclench your jaw. Open your fists. Allow your shoulders to melt down into your back pockets. Release and cleanse to give your body the space it needs for all the "new" that's asking to be absorbed.

THE HEALTHY GODMOTHER HINT: Speaking of cleansing, this would also be a great time for a Device Detox. Remove social media apps from your phone. No phones at the dinner table. Keep phone charging downstairs, not on your bedside table. Use the Do Not Disturb/Airplane Mode features more often. Commit to checking email 3-4 times a day rather than 3-4 times an hour. Try it. Be more present in your life. See if you can cut your usage in half. Watch what happens.

FOODS THAT NOURISH:

- Squashes
- Sweet Potato
- Carrots, beets, parsnips
- Brussel Sprouts

CHAKRAS AT PLAY: Root

SEASONAL FOCUS:

- Nourishing lungs & large intestines
- Prepping for Winter
- Beginning to go inward

RECIPES:

- ACV Spritzer
- Cranberry Flush
- Pineapple Mango Salsa
- Moon Juice Smoothie

JOURNAL THIS:

WHAT HAVE I MADE SO VITAL, VALUABLE, AND REAL ABOUT MY POINT OF VIEW THAT KEEPS ME FROM HAVING MORE JOY? WHAT IS THE VALUE OF PLAY?

Love this information? Get your own private reading or consultation by visiting the writers' personal websites which can be found in the back of The Energy Almanac.

 www.shopBigSky.com

October Notes

November

PROVOCATION. FAMILY. FUTURE. FOUNDATION.

NOVEMBER 2-8
Do wait for clarity before responding.
Don't relive old patterns and habits.

NOVEMBER 9-15
Do be empathetic.
Don't stay focused on what's wrong.

NOVEMBER 16-22
Do take news in stride.
Don't be mediocre.

NOVEMBER 23-29
Do keep a journal and capture new ideas.
Don't be indifferent, be involved.

NOVEMBER 15
NEW MOON IN SCORPIO
Conscious and practical creation.

NOVEMBER 30
FULL MOON LUNAR ECLIPSE IN GEMINI
Juxtaposition of ideas.

November

⋯⋯⋯⋯⋯⋯⋯⋯ ✦ ⋯⋯⋯⋯⋯⋯⋯⋯

PROVOCATION. FAMILY. FUTURE. FOUNDATION.

Unlike some months where many planets are turning retrograde, this month we have three planets - Mercury, Mars, and Neptune - all turning back to forward motion. This picks up the speed of change, delivering you the opportunity to retrace your steps but to see possibility with new eyes.

Likely this will be an emotionally provocative month. The Moon as she moves through Aries and Libra will challenge the Capricorn planets, and when she is in Cancer she will oppose them. Mercury turning direct in Libra also squares the Capricorn planets, Mars in Aries in retrograde and then in direct motion will also square them. These are titanic forces changing the face of the world. There is every reason to be emotionally provoked, but the most important thing to do is be wise about how you go about expressing your emotions. Respond don't react.

DATES TO WATCH:

- **November 3, Election Day in USA. Mercury turns direct in Libra.** Miscommunication possible; use diplomatic speech with one another.

- **November 10, Mercury back into Scorpio.** Deep, passionate, and possibly intense communication.

- **November 13, Mars turns direct in Aries.** Any activity that has been stalled picks up new energy and steam to move forward again.

- **November 14-15, New Moon-Super Moon in Scorpio.** Scorpio urges you to go deeper to connect with what you truly desire. See November Moons below.

- **November 21, Venus into Scorpio.** Venus is sexy, passionate, and seeks intimacy in Scorpio.

- **November 21, Sun into Sagittarius.** A time to see the "big picture" with optimism.

- **November 28, Neptune direct in Pisces.** Moving outward into the world with new insights.

- **November 29/30, Full Moon lunar eclipse in Gemini.** See November Moons below.

ASTROLOGY BY THE WEEKS:

WEEK 1: NOVEMBER 2–8, 2020

The first full week of November is transit quiet. The Moon moves through Taurus, Gemini, Cancer, and Leo. The only transit this week is Mercury square Saturn.

The Moon is in Gemini squaring Neptune in Pisces, resulting in many words flowing on Election Day in the United States. There will be mixed messages you'll hear because of Neptune's and Mercury's change of direction. It may take a few days to get to the truth of the outcome of the elections.

Mid-week through Saturday morning, the Moon will transit through Cancer and oppose the triple conjunction planets in Capricorn. Emotions are running high, making it difficult to think clearly and communicate what you really want to say. Wait for clarity and less emotion.

Shadow: Repeating past mistakes. This particular shadow speaks to your ability to learn from the past. Have you ever heard the saying "history repeats itself"? Can you see the pattern with enough consciousness to disrupt it if necessary, or will you succumb to reliving the old. Recognize what is good, valuable, and worthy from the past and combine it with the highest and best potential for the future.

WEEK 2: NOVEMBER 9–15, 2020

We begin the week with Venus opposing Mars and the Sun trine Neptune, setting the tone for conflict and revelations. Mercury moves forward into Scorpio, Jupiter conjuncts Pluto, Mars turns forward in Aries, while the Moon is in Libra challenging him. The week ends with a New Moon in Scorpio while the Sun is making positive contacts with Pluto and Jupiter, followed the next day by Venus challenging both Pluto and Jupiter.

This is going to be one of those up and down kind of weeks. Venus opposing Mars attempts to be conciliatory and tactful, but Mars is still in a passive-aggressive state. Watch that dynamic in your own personal relationships as well. The Sun trine Neptune shines light on your deeper motivations and perhaps reveals to you some previously unknown truth.

Mercury moving forward through Scorpio is passionate and intense. Here is another possible passive-aggressive tendency. Watch your words. With Mercury back in Scorpio, words can empower or be used as swords to cut. Focus on empathy, care, and being responsible in what you say or do.

Thursday is the next Jupiter-Pluto conjunction in Capricorn followed by Mars turning direct in Aries. There may be trouble in moving forward in these transits. Creating a new established order that is sustainable yet growth supportive is challenging and takes time. Mars could be impatient to get moving and shaking while the Jupiter-Pluto conjunction is more conservative. Be patient with yourself and others now.

We end the week with the New Moon in Scorpio (See November Moons below.) The New Moon is the bright spot this week, but it also presents us with the challenge to let go of drama and move forward as individuals, as a nation, and as a planet. Let's move out of the darkness and into the light.

Shadow: Focusing on the negative. The shadow this week is about turning the corner into the light and the need for us to let go of pessimism, control, and focus on the negative. Bringing in more light means you focus on what is good in the world, express gratitude, and show love and compassion to your fellow human beings.

Week 3: November 16–22, 2020

This week Mercury opposes Uranus, the Sun sextiles Saturn, and Venus squares Saturn. The highlight of the week is the Sun's move into Sagittarius and Venus' move into Scorpio.

Midweek, the Moon is moving through Capricorn, conjuncting the triple conjunction which means emotions probably will be triggered for each of us. There may also be some surprising announcements or disturbing news. Take everything in stride as everything really is unfolding just as it is meant to.

Enthusiasm and optimism may return later in the week when the Sun moves into Sagittarius. Sagittarius energy is forward-looking and boldly adventurous. This is a time of year when we are looking ahead to the new year and to finishing our current projects. Sagittarius is ruled by the planet Jupiter which is currently in a triple conjunction with Pluto and Saturn in Capricorn. You can feel the optimism of the new calling. Remember to stay in the present. Look ahead, yes, but take care of the business in the now. Living in the now with Venus moving into Scorpio means concentrating your energy on what you are passionate about. For the next few weeks, align your life with the values that you most resonate with. Live, love, and breathe your passions.

Shadow: Choosing mediocrity. You may have received messages in the past that it wasn't okay to stand out in the crowd so perhaps you've settled for mediocrity instead of the stellar expression of who you are. Choose now to express the exquisite uniqueness of you.

Week 4: November 23–29, 2020

The week begins with the Moon in Pisces. You may be super sensitive, intuitive, and emotional. The week progresses to the Moon in Aries where there are challenges being raised to the Capricorn triple conjunction planets. On Friday, the Moon conjuncts Uranus and opposes Venus. Even though this is Black Friday, expect conservative spending by everyone. Saturday, spiritual planet Neptune turns direct and the week ends with a lack of clarity about the future.

Watch your dreams and intuition as the week starts. We are super tuned in to imagery, information, and the call of our subconscious or even the superconscious minds. Keep a journal close by to note your inklings and revelations.

Thanksgiving in the United States occurs this week with the Moon in Aries. You know how family gatherings can sometimes trigger us to say or do things we wouldn't normally do or say? There is potential for that on Thursday. Stay in love, and if you can't, then go outside and take a breath.

Saturday Neptune turns direct and you may be feeling less sure of and clear about the future. If you have been following the path of your intuition and inner guidance, you will be in the right place at the right time with the right people and the right opportunity. However, with Neptune turning direct, you may also discover that not listening to your intuition has cost you. Don't beat yourself up. Use this as a lesson learned about how to tune in to your inner guidance now and in the future.

Shadow: The shadow this week feels like the next level of last week's shadow of mediocrity. This shadow sucks the life out of the world we live in. It sits by while others suffer and shrugs its shoulders, saying, "What can I do about it?" The shadow of indifference stops us from claiming and living our passions. Stand up and be different.

....

November Moons

NEW MOON @ 23° SCORPIO | NOVEMBER 15, AT 12:08 AM ET

MOON MUSINGS:

This month, the preponderance of energies in the New Moon are focused on Cardinal Earth. Cardinal Earth is initiating energy. You're getting a real boost in the beginning of this Moon cycle to rapidly and consciously create your reality.

To be sure, there are challenges inherent in this Moon as well. Mars is still stirring the pot, making sure that any changes you make are dynamic and forceful. During the New Moon he is opposing Venus who is exacting a moderating force on him. She seems to whisper, "Action yes, but be aligned with your desires and values." Don't be afraid to set big intentions but be sure they are down-to-earth, practical, and achievable.

One side note to this New Moon. There are a lot of planets at the 23rd degree in the chart (Sun and Moon at 23 Scorpio, Eris at 23 Aries, and Pluto, Jupiter, and Pallas Athene at 23 Capricorn). As any numerologist could tell you, 23 is a 5 (2+3=5) and that is a number of change and the constructive use of freedom. This is simply more indication of powerful new beginnings!!

FULL MOON-LUNAR ECLIPSE @ 9° GEMINI | NOVEMBER 30, AT 4:30 AM ET

MOON MUSINGS:
By the time of the Full Moon lunar eclipse in Gemini, you may be shedding resistance and blocks to moving forward. While this is a releasing time, there is also the opportunity to fix your focus on what you hold dear to you, unless of course, you are still stubbornly holding onto the past?

Such an interesting juxtaposition this Moon puts us in. On the one hand, Gemini and Sagittarius (Moon and Sun respectively) are change agents, while the vast number of planets in Earth evoke stability and staying power. These situations are conundrums that present us with two truths. It is up to us to manage them in a way that, in this instance, is preparing us to move on. Change and stability is needed. Creating a way forward that includes both will be the challenge.

. . . .

Resources

NUMEROLOGY: 6 UNIVERSAL MONTH IN A 4 UNIVERSAL YEAR

KEY WORDS: FAMILY, FUTURE, FOUNDATION
This month will be a very similar energy to that of February 2020. The 6 universal month will attract a focus on the family while the 4 universal year will create the need for a plan relating to your domestic life. This would be a great year to welcome a new baby into your home. Maybe it's time for your parents to move in with you. The family unit is likely to experience some changes this year. This can be the actual family or the family dwelling. This is a great year to secure a good mortgage for that property you want. It is also a great year for renovations. This might be the year where one of the kids leaves home. The foundation of your home is changing. Planning for the future is on the agenda. Remember to try and balance your need to do the right thing with the need to develop a plan or system for your life.

GEMSTONE WISDOM: TREE AGATE
Be like a tree – grounded, secure, and stable. Tree Agate, or dendritic agate, promotes a solid foundation, a calmness, and composure which are all handy tools to have when you are relating to your family. Embrace the peace and tranquility this gemstone provides, particularly when emotional buttons get pushed. Just like a tree has its roots firmly planted into the earth, you too can tap into the grounding energy.

ESSENTIAL OIL APPLICATION:
November brings our awareness to family, future, and foundation. As you cultivate your intentions this month, remember that emotions can run high and extra support could be needed in the areas

✵ www.shopBigSky.com ✵

of communication and trust. Nourish your compassion. Listen deeply to others. It has been said if you want something, give it away. Bringing your attention back to love, you are encouraged to give it away. If you have been cautious or guarded with your feelings, you may decide it is time to dissolve the wall or barrier that was created from past experiences. Love is truly the foundation of trust. Kindness doesn't cost a thing, and your benevolent acts can greatly impact your recipients. The preferred oils this month are just what you need to usher in these positive actions and proceed forward with an authentic open heart.

- **Lavender -** Apply 2 drops to your heart/chest area to facilitate an open heart and clear communication. Put one drop behind the ears to encourage listening and trust. Lavender is one of the gentlest essential oils, yet provides powerful results. Aiding in trust, this oil is your go-to for forgiving yourself and others, genuinely supporting the perfect space for all that needs nurturing.

- **Rose -** 2 drops over heart/chest area to radiate love. One drop on pulse points on neck and each wrist. Unconditional love and compassion is the hallmark for Rose essential oil. Not to be confused with Rose absolute, the highly sought-after Rose essential oil has some of the most profound benefits that can be found. Encouraging compassion and empathy is just what you need to support areas of family, friends, and connection with others. Rose allows acceptance in yourself and others and offers a supportive heart to lead you into the future you desire.

Chakras supported by these oils: Crown, Brow, Heart, Root

Positive Affirmation/Intention:
I embrace and radiate love and kindness. I listen to others with an open heart.

Movement of the Month: Breathwork and Meditation

Our breath is the life force that connects us to our essence of gratitude. This month the movement will be focusing on breath. Each moment can change with your intention and focus. The energy of this month is connecting to gratitude and the many blessings you have. We will add to our practice a rooted meditation posture. Each day, set aside time to root down in your sits bones and connect to the grounding balance of earth. Allow your breath to rise up and behind your spine between the shoulder blades and out through the crown of the head, surrounding you in divine white light.

Create your intention by focusing on gratitude. Release all fears. Inhale... slow, soft, and steady... exhale. Cultivate being detached from your thoughts, letting them float by like clouds without judgment. Find peace as you release control of situations. Sitting in this blessed space, we rewire our brains to be filled with a light that we can share out in the world. Share your gift of gratitude with others!

NOURISHMENT:

Take a dog for a walk in the woods and they will sniff as they go. They mostly intuitively know what is food and what is not. They were born with an inner guidance system that lets them know what they need and when they need it. You were born with the same ability, but with food drizzled in multicolored sprinkles and fast food burgers on every corner, our brains make all the choices rather than our deep levels of intuition. Remember the Self-Trust Jar from June's moon cycle? This is one of the ways this work supports your Nourishment Practice. You learn to remember that you are trustworthy in all areas of your life. You've been told by the $65 Billion Diet Industry that you can't trust yourself around food. It's. A. Lie.

You can trust yourself. It takes practice, self compassion and 100% self acceptance. You are the only one who can determine what's best for you and your unique body composition, history and lifestyle. This is called Bio-Individuality and all nourishment practices that last are built on this foundation, but getting to this point, as you can see, is a process in and of itself.

Keep going. Tap in. Ask and listen. The truth lies with you. As A Course In Miracles says, "The World needs help and God sent YOU!"

THE HEALTHY GODMOTHER HINT: Tis the season for Gratitude. Start a new journal and every night after your Hot Towel Scrub*, (see December) write down three things you are grateful for. If more gratitudes come, great, but start with three. You can also write down things that have not yet come to fruition, and feel the joy as though they already have. Watch it manifest before your eyes. It's like magic!

FOODS THAT NOURISH:

- Whatever intuitively feels good
- Throat Coat Tea

SEASONAL FOCUS:

- Warming
- Intuitive Eating
- Nourishing Lungs & Large Intestines

CHAKRAS AT PLAY: Root, Sacral, Throat

RECIPES:

- Coconut Custard Pie
- Chocolate Flourless Torte

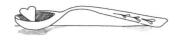

JOURNAL THIS:

WHAT IF ME BEING ME IS A HUGE CONTRIBUTION TO THE WORLD? WHAT CAN I BE, KNOW, PERCEIVE OR RECEIVE THAT IF I WERE TO BE, KNOW, PERCEIVE OR RECEIVE IT WOULD CHANGE EVERYTHING FOR ME?

Love this information? Get your own private reading or consultation by visiting the writers' personal websites which can be found in the back of The Energy Almanac.

November Notes

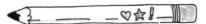

_____
_____
_____
_____
_____
_____
_____
_____
_____
_____
_____
_____
_____
_____
_____
_____
_____
_____
_____
_____
_____
_____
_____
_____
_____
_____
_____
_____

Energy Almanac   2020 Edition

December

OPTIMISM. SELF. SOUL-SEARCHING. SECLUSION.

NOVEMBER 30–DECEMBER 6

DO EMBRACE YOUR OWN EVOLUTION.
DON'T BE REACTIVE.

DECEMBER 7–13

DO SEEK WAYS TO BE PEACEFUL.
DON'T GET CAUGHT UP IN RHETORIC.

DECEMBER 14–20

DO HAVE HEALTHY BOUNDARIES.
DON'T BE RIGID IN YOUR THINKING.

DECEMBER 21–27

DO HONOR THE WINTER SOLSTICE.
DON'T ALLOW YOUR POINT OF VIEW TO DISTORT REALITY.

DECEMBER 28–JANUARY 3, 2021

DO COME INTO ALIGNMENT WITH LOVE,
FORGIVENESS, AND COMPASSION. DON'T AVOID QUIET REFLECTION.

A CHANGE IN DIRECTION

NEW MOON SOLAR ECLIPSE

SHHH... SEEKING PEACE

go in

JOURNAL

DECEMBER 14
NEW MOON SOLAR ECLIPSE IN SAGITTARIUS
EVOLUTIONARY IMPULSES.

DECEMBER 29
FULL MOON IN CANCER
INDEPENDENT MOTIVATION TO CHANGE.

Energy Almanac 2020 Edition

 www.shopBigSky.com

December

······· ✬ ·······

OPTIMISM. SELF. SOUL SEARCHING. SECLUSION.

While all our troubles, transformation, and chaos are not completely over, December has a much more hopeful feel to it. Optimism is one of the hallmarks of Sagittarius and for most of the month of December, we have the Sun, Mercury, and Venus in Sagittarius buoying us up. The grander cycles of time move on in the background, with a new Great Conjunction of Jupiter and Saturn at zero Aquarius added to the fun. It is distinctly possible that we can find hope and optimism this month.

Jupiter-Saturn in Aquarius also presents humanity with challenges. For this month, enjoy the quieter energy. Rest, restore, and renew!

DATES TO WATCH:

- **December 1, Mercury into Sagittarius.** Thinking and speaking in broad, optimistic terms.

- **December 14, New Moon Solar Eclipse in Sagittarius.** See December Moons below.

- **December 15, Venus into Sagittarius.** Universal love, romantic adventures, and truth in your relationships take center stage.

- **December 16, Saturn into Aquarius.** Building an innovative future with eccentric intelligence.

- **December 19, Jupiter into Aquarius.** The return of tolerance and inclusiveness.

- **December 20, Mercury into Capricorn.** Speaking clearly, thinking logically, and setting goals to live by.

- **December 21, Sun into Capricorn and Winter Solstice.** Focus on goals with a realistic and grounded approach to life.

- **December 21, Jupiter conjunct Saturn.** Called a "Great Conjunction" as it happens only every 18-20 years, the coming together of these two planets sets the social focus for the next two decades.

Energy Almanac 2020 Edition

✬ www.shopBigSky.com ✬

ASTROLOGY BY THE WEEKS:

WEEK 1: NOVEMBER 30 – DECEMBER 6, 2020
There is a Venus trine Neptune transit that reminds us to love unconditionally.

The only irritant in the week is the Moon moving through Cancer squaring Mars and opposing Pluto, Jupiter, and Saturn. By now you are used to this kind of emotional provocation and know how to deal with it appropriately.

Venus in Scorpio trine Neptune in Pisces reminds us of the deeper connection we all share. Though we are different on the outside, we are ultimately all the same. Everyone desires to give and receive love, to belong to a family or community, and to live their lives in freedom. See how we are alike and all deserving of unconditional love.

Shadow: Avoid emotional reactivity. The shadow of emotional immaturity will continue to pop up in your shadow over the next years as you embrace the coming evolution. There is no time like the present to learn to change how we engage our emotions.

WEEK 2: DECEMBER 7–13 , 2020
This week there are a couple of intensely energetic days with Sun square Neptune and Venus sextiles Pluto, Sun trines Mars and squaring Pluto, Jupiter, and Saturn.

There is a spotlight shining on your confusion. Perhaps you discover where you have been duped, misguided, or lied to (either by someone else or by your own self). Now you can take steps to correct. Remember self-love and self-compassion.

On Thursday of this week (December 10), Venus sextiles Pluto, Sun trines Mars and the Moon moves through late Libra opposing Mars and squaring Pluto, Jupiter, and Saturn. Yikes! This might be a difficult day. You may be easily provoked by the rhetoric you hear or by circumstances. You've been through this already a dozen times this year! Be in peace, meditate, turn off the TV and electronic devices, and just chill.

Shadow: Incorrect use of the will. Willpower is quite literally the ability to harness the energy of light to bring about right action, correct thought, and uplifting words. But with the incorrect use of will, we are covertly or maybe overtly manipulative in getting what we want. Often this manipulation feeds into greed and dominance. What would happen if we focused our will on the good for all?

WEEK 3: DECEMBER 14–20, 2020
There is a lot of movement in the heavens this week which has the effect of changing the direction of flow in the energies, and that can make you feel powerless or that things are happening outside of your control.

Energy Almanac 2020 Edition

The week begins with a New Moon Solar Eclipse, then Venus moves into Sagittarius followed by Saturn and Jupiter moving into Aquarius, and at the end of the week Mercury moves into Capricorn.

A New Moon Solar Eclipse is filled with potential. This one in Capricorn shows the potential of working together and working hard on goals, supporting new frameworks.

Venus in Sagittarius takes on universal love. For the next few weeks, we see the bigger picture in our relationships and optimism is restored. Venus also sextiles Saturn now and that means we can more easily see and respect each other's unique points of view.

Saturn and Jupiter both moving into Aquarius in the same week heralds the winds of change in our social and cultural landscape. Idealism, innovation, and invention take center stage. How we can serve the wider world and our fellow human beings comes up for us as individuals now.

Mercury into Capricorn affects the mind and your ability to speak. You have clarity and are able to think and speak in an organized way. You plainly see the pattern of action steps needed in order to achieve a goal.

Shadow: Boundaries, limits, and rigidity. We tend to think of boundaries and limits as not so great, while thinking that limitlessness is good. Structure and form are good. They hold us together as do our skin and bones. The negative impact of becoming rigid is what you need to work with now. Refusing to change or refusing to yield to new energies causes rigidity and stagnation and ultimately death. Have healthy boundaries and set proper limits but be prepared to change when necessary.

Week 4: December 21–27, 2020

This week begins with the Winter Solstice and the Sun's move into Capricorn. We also have Jupiter conjunct Saturn in a transit that will affect the next two decades.

Mars square Pluto this week has a dangerous feel to it, and Mercury trine Uranus has an unpredictable edge. These high energies coming to us just before the Christmas holiday are a bit disturbing, but you have the skills to cope with just about anything.

The Jupiter-Saturn conjunction is much bigger than what can be written here, but the coming together of these two planets sets the social focus for the next two decades. What should we focus on? That is the choice. Innovation, inventions that better our lives, health advances, environmental advances, interpreting laws with more equality. The potential is phenomenal. We each have the power to set the agenda for what we want to see. Get involved in your local efforts to create change.

Mars square Pluto. This aspect isn't so easy. It spells military action or some other kind of volatile situation. Upsetting though this may be, remain calm and focused on the positive if possible. Mercury trine Uranus adds an element of surprising communication to the week. But surprises aren't all bad. Perhaps we hear of a military action that averts a catastrophe? Be prepared for anything.

Shadow: Resisting what is. This is an appropriate shadow to discuss during a week where things may be a little dicey. There is a tendency to view what happens in the world in terms of "good" or "bad." But in reality, the events going on are completely neutral. It is your personal interpretation and emotional response to what is happening that makes the difference. You can choose to resist what is, or just go with the flow.

Week 5: December 28, 2020 – January 3, 2021
There are no major transits ending this most tumultuous year.

Expect a quiet week, though there may be some instability brewing behind the scenes. The only major aspect is a Venus square Neptune, and of course we are again at the Moon in Cancer triggering our Mars, Saturn, and Jupiter. However, there is a big change as Saturn and Jupiter are in a different sign now. The connections are not so charged up; you can breathe and find peace. Venus and Neptune coming together in a square urges you to be more in alignment with spiritual ideals of love, forgiveness, and compassion. What a beautiful ending to 2020 and a great beginning for 2021.

Shadow: Stress and dissatisfaction. You have come through a lot of trauma and drama this year and are used to being on guard. The opposite energies available are bliss and peace. Take your pick.

....

December Moons

NEW MOON–SOLAR ECLIPSE @ 23° SAGITTARIUS | DECEMBER 14, AT 11:17 AM ET

MOON MUSINGS:
The New Moon, empowered by a Solar Eclipse, presents us with potential new beginnings, and this one holds potential for new "evolutionary" impulses to be received by us.

The Sun/Moon conjunction (New Moon) is trine Mars and that means actionable steps are possible. You have the energy and stamina to stick with your intentions until they manifest.

You are also faced with the shadow fear of "not being able to manifest" what you desire. Be sure that your thoughts and emotions are aligned completely with what you want, or you may find yourself with less than satisfactory results. Claim yourself as a master manifester and so it is.

FULL MOON @ 9° CANCER | DECEMBER 29, AT 10:29 PM ET

MOON MUSINGS:

Release, complete, and reveal. That is the energy of any Full Moon. Perhaps you have been feeling like too much is out of your control or maybe you're feeling confused by the whole idea of creating your reality. One thing for sure in this Full Moon is there's one-half of the chart that is empty of planets. It's your job to fill the gap with practical steps to enact your creative energies. It's time to put the pedal to the metal and stop pussyfooting around! Be independent and don't hold yourself back. Soar, grow, evolve, and set your sights on your heart's desires. Move into 2021 with goals and an action plan!

....

Resources

NUMEROLOGY: 7 UNIVERSAL MONTH IN A 4 UNIVERSAL YEAR

KEY WORDS: SELF, SOUL SEARCHING, SECLUSION

This is another 7 universal month in a 4 universal year. This might be a challenge given the holiday season and all. The 7 energy always pulls us inward. This is a time for quiet reflection just when someone is pouring the next rum and eggnog! No doubt you will be jockeying for time by yourself and time with others. Your need to be alone will likely be larger than your need to be with family. How is that even possible?! All things in moderation...even rum balls and family! This will be a great month to work by yourself if possible. You are naturally drawn into your cave this month, but the 4 universal year still has a large focus on work and attention to details. Resist the temptation to over commit this month. See if you can carve out some time to pour into yourself so you can emerge and be the holiday champion.

GEMSTONE WISDOM: RHYOLITE

To thine own self be true. So is the energy of the gemstone Rhyolite. Self-exploration, self-acceptance, and self-love are the attributes of Rhyolite's energy. Who are you, right now, in this present moment? Forget about the past, create your now. Embrace, love, and accept it.

ESSENTIAL OIL APPLICATION:

The month of December is providing us with a wonderful opportunity to reflect and focus on self, soul searching, and conclusion. There are times when pulling back from the noise of it all to realign with our intentions is needed. Taking this time to focus on your own energy and self-care during one of the busiest times of the year is especially important. It can be easy to overextend yourself and take on too much responsibility. Reconnect with the peaceful essence of your being. Journal your thoughts, and release anything that is weighing you down. You will find that using the oils selected for you this month can offer a purifying new start and ease your mind, body, and spirit. What a beautiful way to conclude this year.

- **Frankincense -** Apply 1 drop to brow center (center of forehead) to allow the flow of your creative process and the innate wisdom you have within you to express itself. Frankincense is considered the father of all oils. It imbues strength, feelings of safety, and life stability. Use this oil to harness grounding properties while facilitating your spiritual connectedness to your source. A powerful self-reflection oil, immerse yourself with the giant "soul hug" Frankincense can provide.

- **Reassuring Blend -** A blend of Vetiver, Lavender, Ylang Ylang, Labdanum Leaf, Frankincense, Clary Sage, Marjoram, and Spearmint. Apply this blend on the back of the neck near the base of the hairline/skull and the bottom of the forearm, starting at the wrist and ending on the crease of your arm near the elbow. Reassuring Blend is truly a gift to assist in releasing fear and uncertainty. Feelings of contentment ensue with this blend of oils. For any uneasy feelings that come up for you, melt them away by using this blend. As change occurs in areas of your life, allow this blend of oils to keep you calm through any transitions.

Chakras supported by these oils: Crown, Throat, Heart, Solar Plexus, Sacral, Root

POSITIVE AFFIRMATION/INTENTION:
I trust that everything unfolds as it should. I allow my higher self and divine guidance to illuminate my path.

MOVEMENT OF THE MONTH: MODIFIED SUN SALUTATIONS
December is finding hope and optimism. This month's movement will incorporate the flow of the sunrise polarity posture, a gentle version of a standing modified sun salutations.

Standing with feet hip distance apart, heels toward each other, knees slightly bent, bring your hands to your heart center, palms together, thumbs resting on your breast bone. Our attention is turned inward as we inhale. Hands part and raise toward the sky as the knees straighten. As you exhale, your arms open wide, like a blossoming flower and your head gently tips back; your knees bend, and you feel the expansion of your heart center. Inhale as arms go up again - the knees straighten. As you exhale, your palms touch again and return to your heart center. Complete seven rounds of this series daily, following your inner guidance to increase the number if you feel called to do so. What a divine start to enter 2021 with the feelings of bliss and peace.

Energy Almanac 2020 Edition

NOURISHMENT:

Wow. What a year. While things haven't finished twisting and turning, December promises hope and optimism to round out the year. How appropriate because with the Solstice comes the light!

Speaking of the longest night, the cosmos might be laying off for a bit, but the holidays can also rock your world in ways that leave you reeling. Good quality sleep is critical for being able to keep your nourishment in check so you can set healthy boundaries, reduce emotional reactivity, and channel your willpower to harness the energy you need to wrap up the year with grace.

Create a solid bedtime routine by incorporating foods rich in melatonin and tryptophan like bananas, tomatoes, asparagus, pomegranate, and turkey toward the end of the day. Stay off devices for one hour before bed, and get to bed earlier and/or sleep later. You can also wash off the day with a Hot Towel Scrub*. This ritual involves a plush white wash cloth, a candle, essential oils (optional) and, of course, hot water. Fill sink with steamy hot water, wet towel, and ring mostly dry. Place on face and feel the steam. Breathe in, relax. Continue to wet cloth and move/scrub in circular motions, moving from fingertips and toes toward your heart. Finish by applying your favorite moisturizer. Be with yourself. Practice unconditional love and self-acceptance.

THE HEALTHY GODMOTHER HINT: Did you know that raw cacao (dark chocolate) is rich in stress-reducing and calming magnesium? Listen to your intuition when you find yourself craving chocolate. Let it melt in your mouth. Look for other ways to get more magnesium in your diet with broccoli, almonds, and avocados.

FOODS THAT NOURISH:

- Dark chocolate
- Asparagus
- Tomatoes
- Pomegranate
- Turkey

SEASONAL FOCUS:

- Sleep in heavenly peace
- Winter Solstice-return of the light
- Hibernation

CHAKRAS AT PLAY: Root, Sacral, Solar Plexus

RECIPES:

- Chocolate Flourless Torte
- #betterthan Cookies for Santa
- #betterthan Eggnog Latte

JOURNAL THIS:

WHAT IS THE BENEFIT OF QUIET SECLUSION? WHAT PATTERNS OF HARMONY CAN I BE AND RECEIVE THAT WILL ALLOW PEACE TO BE PRESENT WITH ME?

Love this information? Get your own private reading or consultation by visiting the writer's personal websites which can be found in the back of The Energy Almanac.

 www.shopBigSky.com

December Notes

✩ www.shopBigSky.com ✩

Safe Essential Oil Use

◇ ⬦ ◇

Purchase quality organic, pesticide free, or wild harvested essential oils that have undergone third party GC/MS (Gas Chromatography/Mass Spectrometry) testing from companies who share these results. This information can be found on the oil company's website or printed materials.

Know your oil. Make sure each bottle of essential oil lists most, if not all, of these categories: the Latin name, method of extraction, cultivation, plant part used, country of origin, and distillation date.

Think sustainably. Did you know it takes 30-50 roses to distill one drop of Rose Otto essential oil? That's a lot of plant material for one tiny drop. Buy and use only what you need, reducing consumer waste and protecting the environment for future generations.

Yes, always dilute your essential oils in a carrier before use. A carrier is a liquid or semi-solid usually vegetable-derived base such as Jojoba, Apricot, Olive, Grapeseed, Coconut, even Cocoa Butter. If you're not sure how to dilute oils, see below.

1. **Find your Standard Dilution Rate below for the individual receiving application.**
   - 2 - 6 years old use 1 % dilution
   - 6 - 15 years old use 2 % dilution
   - 15 + years old use 3 % dilution
   - Use 1 % or less for full body application, daily, or long-term use.
   - You can use up to 10% dilution for small areas or acute situations.

2. **Establish how much base/carrier you need.** Are you making a roll on for spot application, or are you making a full body massage oil?

3. **Now that you know the dilution rate and volume of base needed, use the dilution chart below to find out how many drops of essential oils you need** to safely and effectively create an appropriate dilution.

DILUTION CHART
BASE OIL TO ESSENTIAL OIL DROPS

VOLUME OF BASE	0.5%	1%	2%	3%	4%	5%	10%
15 ML (1/2 oz)	2	4	9	13	18	22	44
30 ML (1 oz)	4	9	18	27	36	45	90

✮ www.shopBigSky.com ✮

Energy Almanac 2020 Edition

Keep essential oils away from eyes, ears, and mucous membranes, as most essential oils have the potential to be mucous membrane and skin irritants, especially if they are old or oxidized.

Consult with a certified aromatherapist and/or your healthcare practitioner to evaluate the appropriate selection of an oil, dilution rate, method of use, duration of use, potential drug interactions, or contraindications before using essential oils for the following:

- For internal use. Essential Oils are highly concentrated botanicals that deserve safe care and handling and have potential for adverse reactions.
- If pregnant, breastfeeding, or under the age of three.
- If severely ill, elderly, undergoing surgery, taking multiple medications or diagnosed with Hypertension or Epilepsy.

To learn more about safe and effective essential oil use through maternity, motherhood and for women's health, contact Stephanie Veilleux-Welch: Certified Aromatherapist & Childbirth Doula at **www.LavendoulaME.com**

Writers

◇◆◇

TAM VEILLEUX, Virgo extraordinaire, is a coach and creative. As a graphic recorder and illustrator, her goal is to make information easy to remember through her light-hearted approach to sketching. She also provides group and private coaching using a holistic energetic approach. Fun, fresh transformation is the crux of her online boutique of products and services that will help you create real and lasting change.

> **Contact:** Tam@choosebigchange.com visit: www.shopBigSky.com
> on Instagram @Shop.Big.Sky

JANET HICKOX, Gemini, is an intuitive astrologer and Human Design coach whose point of difference is the ability to take a complex subject like astrology and break it down into a language that everyone understands. Her philosophy is simple. She wants you to understand and be able to interact on the subject of you. A living astrology reading unlocks key personality characteristics that may be lying dormant and that make you your unique self. Janet can teach you to tap into those characteristics so you can assist yourself in life's opportunities or challenges in any life area. Discover the power of a personal astrology reading.

> **Contact:** janet@living-astrology.com, follow on Instagram @janorama_2011
> or visit www.living-astrology.com

ANN PERRY, Aries, has committed a third of her life to helping people reconnect to their soul's contract through numerology readings, workshops, and courses. There is no bigger thrill for Ann than to help you identify what the heck you are here for on this planet. Contact Ann for your own private reading and to learn more on how your personal numbers are impacting you.

> **Contact:** ann@annperrynumerologist.com visit: www.annperrynumerologist.com

LISA FONTANELLA, Taurus. You can never have too many rocks! That is Lisa Fontanella's motto. Her fascination with rocks has taken on many forms, much like the rocks she holds so dear. She creates jewelry using gemstones, writes stories for children about the wonders of rocks, and gets so excited when she sees a type of rock she has never seen before. A wanna-be rock hound, Lisa loves learning about rocks, their properties, and feeling their energy. This love is evident in her first children's book, Crystal's Quest: An Adventure into the World of Gemstones (available at Amazon). This sweet and educational book was an award-winning Finalist in the Children's Mind/Body/Spirit category of the 2019 International Book Awards. Lisa is also a Reiki master (27 years and counting!), holistic practitioner, and certified Life Coach.

> **Contact:** www.LisaFontanella.com

STARLA PERICO, Virgo, is a Holistic Practitioner, international speaker, and essential oil educator. As an energy worker, intuitive healer, and empath, she has almost two decades of experience. Certified in many holistic modalities, the passion she holds is to help others be the best version of themselves. Educating and supporting individuals and groups worldwide with the uses of essential oils for emotional health and overall well-being is the foundation of her service to others. As a doTERRA Gold Leader, she inspires others to use essential oils every day in every way.

Contact: Starla@nurturewithoils.com or visit her website: www.nurturewithoils.com

PENNY ELLIS, Virgo, began her journey to gather knowledge and wisdom in order to learn and share the modalities of alternative healing after experiencing the therapeutic touch of a Reiki session during a chronic illness. She is a graduate of Holistic Alternatives, certified in Polarity Therapy, and has an art level in Reiki. Penny completed a 200-hour yoga training and has continued to deepen that education. She is also a Wellness Consultant with DoTERRA CPTG essential oils, incorporating essential oils into her work and daily life. She strives to create a space for healing and peaceful insight in her sessions and yoga classes. She enjoys nature and remaining active in the lives of her children and grandchildren along with her husband Brad and two beautiful labs. Contact Penny to schedule a session or find her current yoga schedule.

Contact: Instagram at @Yogagrammi or at penny@bhsinc.net

HEIDI SYMONDS, Aquarius, also known as The Healthy Godmother, is a holistic lifestyle coach, spiritual mentor and intuitive marketing co-creator on a mission to help women stand in their power, speak their truth and own their worth while they manifest their dreams and create life changing impact to those around them. She guides them in using food and love to look and more importantly FEEL amazing with her bite size strategies and validating encouragement. If you are looking for #betterthan recipes or a Business Bestie to help you take the next step in your life or biz contact her at her website.

Contact: www.HeidiSymonds.com

STEPHANIE VEILLEUX–WELCH, Aquarius, is a certified aromatherapist and childbirth doula who cares deeply about the proper use and application of essential oils. To learn more about safe and effective essential oil use through maternity, motherhood, and for women's health, contact Stephanie today.

Contact: www.LavendoulaME.com

LOVE THE Energy Almanac?

SHARE YOUR LOVE

ON SOCIAL MEDIA WITH THESE HASHTAGS

#EnergyAlmanac

#MagicMaker

#2019TEA

Get your 2021 Almanac here: **www.shopBigSky.com**

JOIN US AT MAGIC MAKER'S PLACE ON FACEBOOK FOR MORE FUN, FRESH, TRANSFORMATIONAL INFORMATION.

Reach the publisher, Tam Veilleux, by email:
Tam@choosebigchange.com

 www.shopBigSky.com

PLAN BY THE PLANETS & ADD PERSONAL DEVELOPMENT PRACTICES INTO EVERY DAY!

INCLUDE MIND-SET DEVELOPMENT EVERY DAY.
GAIN CLARITY, CONFIDENCE, AND MOMENTUM.
KEEP YOUR SCHEDULE STRAIGHT.

THIS IS A RESOURCE BOOK FOR SCHEDULING AND PERSONAL DEVELOPMENT.

This Magic Makers PLANNER & PLAYBOOK is perfect for you:

- More than 200 fresh-sketched powerful pages!
- The power of asking generative questions but prefer someone else write them for you.
- Goal setting is on your mind but you don't have a clear system for writing them or remembering them.
- Self-help and personal development is something you value but you fall off the wagon regularly.
- You love writing in a calendar to keep track of all of your crazy cool dates, appointments and events.
- You're learning a little about the energies of astrology, the moons and numerology and want to grow that knowledge base and incorporate it into your monthly routines.
- You value deepening your understanding of connecting to energy and using it for momentum.
- You appreciate fun and you are smitten with color, wit and quotes that make you think.
- Coloring is your jam. These pages just beg you to add color to them.
- Order your Magic Makers Planner + Playbook at: **www.shopBigSky.com**.

 ✳ www.shopBigSky.com ✳

CPSIA information can be obtained
at www.ICGtesting.com
Printed in the USA
BVHW021654280120
570620BV00040B/2253